Michael
Scott-Joynt

J... Bob Morgan

Lent 1992

Women and Religion Series

Series Editor: Dr Janet Martin Soskice

Women Priests?, ed. Alyson Peberdy

After Eve

edited by

Janet Martin Soskice

Collins
Marshall Pickering

Text set in Baskerville by Avocet Robinson, Buckingham
Printed in Great Britain by Cox & Wyman Ltd, Reading, Berks.

Contents

Series Introduction

Theology, writes the German theologian, J.-B. Metz, 'must again and again be interrupted by praxis and experience. The important questions to be asked by theology, then, are: Who should do theology and where, in whose interest and for whom?'[1]

Women, one assumes, have always been religious, but women have not always written theology. Indeed, if one is considering theology as an academic discipline (certainly not the only definition) then women have only been admitted in any numbers to universities as students of theology since the Second World War.

A remarkable feature of the theological scene in recent years thus has been the steady increase of writings by women on religious matters, and writings about women in religious faith and life. Almost inevitably, many of these writings are by new pens and have appeared in journals of limited circulation. Yet it is sometimes at such edges and not from the heartlands that the faith grows. This series hopes to bring works of importance to wider audiences.

The Women and Religion series has as its broad brief to publish writings of religious importance by women and/or about the place of women in the world's faiths. Some of these writings may recognisably be formal theology, some may not, and some may challenge the distinction of what counts as theology and who is a theologian in the first place.

Dr Janet Martin Soskice
The Divinity School, Cambridge University

[1] J.-B. Metz, *Faith in History and Society* (London: Burns & Oates, 1980), p. 58.

The Contributors

There are few women academic theologians in Britain and consequently few individuals for whom 'women' is *the* main academic interest. Britain does possess, however, a number of excellent theologians who wish to make some contribution to this debate. All the contributors, male and female, are well known authorities and authors of important recent books.

Paul Joyce is a Lecturer in Old Testament Studies at the University of Birmingham. He is the Secretary of the Society for the Study of the Old Testament and author of *Divine Initiative and Human Response in Ezekiel* (Sheffield, 1989).

Robert Morgan is a Lecturer in New Testament Theology and Fellow of Linacre College, Oxford. He is co-author (with John Barton) of *Biblical Interpretation* (Oxford, 1988). He is also editor of *The Religion of the Incarnation* (Bedminster, 1989).

Léonie Archer is a member of Wolfson College, Oxford and until 1989 was Fellow in Jewish Studies of the Greco-Roman Period at the Oxford Centre for Postgraduate Hebrew Studies. She is author of *Her Price is Beyond Rubies: The Jewish Woman in Graeco-Roman Palestine* (Sheffield, 1990).

Timothy Radcliffe OP taught theology for many years at Blackfriars, Oxford and has been a frequent contributor to *New Blackfriars*. He is Provincial of the Dominicans of Great Britain.

Sebastian Brock is Reader in Aramaic and Syriac at the Oriental Institute of Oxford University and co-author (with Susan Ashbrook Harvey) of *Holy Women of the Syrian Orient* (Berkeley, 1987).

Jane Barr is a classicist with a special interest in St Jerome. She is a Lecturer in Church History at Vanderbilt University.

Sister Benedicta Ward is a member of the Anglican religious community of the Sisters of the Love of God, author of a number of books and articles of early and medieval spirituality, and teaches in Oxford.

Stephen Sykes is the Bishop of Ely and was formerly Regius Professor of Divinity at Cambridge University. He is the author of many books.

Paul S. Fiddes is the Principal of Regent's Park College in the University of Oxford and teaches Christian doctrine. He is a Minister in the Baptist Union of Great Britain and author of *The Creative Suffering of God* (Oxford, 1988) and *Past Event and Present Salvation: The Christian Idea of Atonement* (London, 1989).

Ann Loades is Senior Lecturer in Theology at the University of Durham. Formerly co-presenter of Channel 4's '7 Days', she is author of *Searching for Lost Coins* (London, 1987), and editor of *Feminist Theology: A Reader* (London, 1990) and has taught feminist theology in Britain and America.

Introduction to the Essays

The collection falls into three sections on a historical basis: Biblical, Patristic/Medieval, and Modern.

Paul Joyce provides an introduction to feminist reading of the Old Testament, both its goals and its pitfalls. He guides one clearly through the central literature and makes particular reference to the issue of biblical authority.

Robert Morgan shows, with reference to the New Testament, that interpretations of the Bible are aspects of the wider task of 'doing theology'; that all interpretations of Scripture are theological interpretations. He discusses the relationship between belief and values, particularly in the case of feminist interpretation, although he insists that his own is not a piece of feminist theology. Special attention is devoted to Paul.

Léonie Archer's essay is an example of a critical scholarly approach to some difficult biblical material on the relation in Judaism between blood and purity. She charts, within Judaism of her period, a developing exclusion of women, both social and religious, and makes an original connection between the shedding of blood in circumcision and in menstruation.

Timothy Radcliffe has written a clear and delightful exposition of 1 Corinthians 11.2–6, a passage focused on bodiliness, sexual identity and grace, using recent New Testament material. The article is an excellent example of how a scholar can bring the fruits of scholarship to a non-scholarly audience.

The same can be said for *Sebastian Brock*. The word for 'spirit' is feminine in Semitic language, a grammatical fact that had theological repercussions for the Syriac churches of the first four Christian centuries. Notably, the third person of the Trinity was regularly personified in female terms. Dr Brock discusses this, and the reasons for change in practice in the fifth and sixth centuries.

Jane Barr gives a useful and sympathetic account of one of the most influential and misogynistic of the Church Fathers, Jerome. Jerome was the translator of the Vulgate, the chief version of the Bible in use throughout medieval Europe. He made a few mistakes, but a disproportionately large number of these come in passages dealing with women where inevitably Jerome's direction was to make the text harsher. His embellishment of Genesis 3.16 is of 'almost unquantifiable importance' to subsequent Catholic discussions of female subordination.

None the less, as *Benedicta Ward*'s paper illustrates, the medieval period saw a number of outstanding women mystics and religious. Such female 'visionaries' were often contrasted to male 'theologians'. Sr Benedicta contrasts one such visionary, Hildegard of Bingen, with the more analytic mysticism of Teresa of Avila four hundred years later, and asks what accounts for the changes.

Richard Hooker wrote his influential works in the sixteenth century from within the newly reformed English Church, yet his works have continuing importance, especially within Anglicanism. *The Bishop of Ely, Stephen Sykes* discusses directions Hooker provides for a distinctly Anglican way forward on the ordination of women. Hooker, despite the negative views on women he would have shared with Elizabethan contemporaries, shows a vision of a 'discipleship of equals' to be at the heart of the nature of the Church.

Paul Fiddes brings us to the twentieth century with discussion of the Reformed theologian, Karl Barth, some would say the most important theologian of the century. Barth is (in)famous for remarks on the subordination of women, but Fiddes shows that Barth's views are not crudely hierarchical, and that much of value remains with his use of the category of 'covenant' between male and female, God and man. This more positive assessment of Barth is welcome although certain to be controversial.

Ann Loades writes about 'Mary' and the cult of Mary from a feminist and detached perspective. Her discussion, however, is both ecumenical and judicious, considering Papal Encyclicals and recent Catholic texts, before discussing the feminist literature on Mary and reaching her own conclusions.

Editor's Introduction

Women are writing about theology – this much many people know. But what have theologians written about women? A glib answer would be that, in nearly two thousand years of Christian history, women have been discussed relatively rarely. While great theologians of the past might have written volumes on the Trinity or atonement, or the inspiration of scripture, 'woman' arises only incidentally as a topic in their works. And this one might expect, for the important focus when talking specifically about human beings has been on what has been called until recently, 'the Christian doctrine of Man', with 'man' understood as a term embracing both sexes. What goes for men in theology then would seem to go for women and there is no need to discuss women separately.

But does what goes for men, go for women? Not always, apparently. Where one finds 'woman' discussed in the historical literature it is often to express the view that although *for the most part* men and women are the same 'in the sight of God', in some important ways they are not. As to why women are different, or how they are different, or how they should be different there is much disagreement – not least today. What then does it mean to be a woman in the Jewish or Christian tradition, a woman 'after Eve'?

The essays in this collection are not for the most part essays in feminist theology, at least not in the sense of overtly advancing the cause of women. They are, however, essays by scholars persuaded of the importance of the issues raised by modern feminist thought, and able to display some of the richness and ambiguity of the western religious traditions to which we, whether we be religious or not, are heirs.

The essays are arranged in a loosely historical order, but need not necessarily be read in that order. Indeed, the first two essays, by Paul Joyce and Robert Morgan, might as easily have been last since both deal with *contemporary* feminist biblical interpretation.

Readers unfamiliar with the topics under discussion may wish to start with the essays of Jane Barr or Timothy Radcliffe, both of whom with a light yet scholarly touch, help to show the problems unavoidably present in our inherited traditions of reading and even of translating the biblical books.

The historically inclined may look to the essays of Léonie Archer, Sebastian Brock and Benedicta Ward which show, in one way or another, that far from being a constant, the place of women and the appraisal of the feminine within the Jewish and Christian religious traditions varies considerably over time – sometimes in directions hostile to women's equality, and sometimes in directions favouring it.

Those interested in contemporary responses, and in ways in which a modern theologian might try to re-evaluate (and even challenge) the tradition in which she or he stands, will find in Stephen Syke's essay a lively defence of the Anglican tradition as grounded in the past but free to act in ways fitting to new circumstances; free for instance to ordain women. Paul Fiddes pushes Karl Barth further down an egalitarian road than that author might have intended or wishes, basing his argument on Barth's own doctrine of the Trinity. And Ann Loades, in an amusing and perceptive essay, looks through non-Roman Catholic feminist eyes at the place of Mary in Christian thought and devotion, and comes to the conclusion that, with certain caveats, Mary may still have something to offer to the feminist quest.

I very much hope that those readers who are not students or teachers of theology may enjoy this opportunity to join the historian, or linguist, or theologian in their work shops and see how unexpected areas of academic expertise may be brought to bear on contemporary problems and especially our chosen one of women after Eve.

Janet Martin Soskice
Jesus College, Cambridge

Feminist Exegesis of the Old Testament: Some Critical Reflections

Paul Joyce

The question of how we are to understand and interpret Scripture, in all its diversity, across a broad cultural divide is one of the central and perennial issues of theology. One area in which this is keenly felt in some contemporary Christian circles is that relating to women and the feminine. Feminist exegesis of the Bible, though having roots at least as early as the work of Elizabeth Cady Stanton in the nineteenth century,[1] has been an increasingly significant feature of the theological scene in recent years. This form of criticism may seem rather alien to those accustomed to more traditional approaches, but its challenges and insights need to be taken seriously by all, not least because they often raise in sharp form many questions which are of importance to biblical interpretation as a whole, including those which relate to the authority of Scripture. In this short essay, we shall consider some of the key issues raised, in specific relation to the Old Testament.

There is, of course, much in the Old Testament which presents a decidedly 'negative' view of women. As an example we may cite the presentation of sinful Israel as a dissolute woman in Ezekiel chapter sixteen, or again the image of the harlot as the embodiment of folly in Proverbs chapter seven. There have been a number of different responses to such material. Throughout much of Christian tradition, the tendency has often been for 'negative' biblical themes concerning women to be given prominence – for example, the part played by the woman in the garden of Eden.[2] Such an emphasis has often both been informed by and in turn sanctioned the assumptions of Church and society regarding the place and role of women. Needless to say, traditional views of this kind have generally gone together with an assumption that a high degree of authority is to be attributed to the canon of Scripture.

At another extreme, we find the so-called post-Christian feminists such as Mary Daly or, in Britain, Daphne Hampson.[3] Their position shares with most traditional interpretation the general supposition that the biblical witness with regard to women is essentially negative. Indeed, these critics have helped us see much more clearly the extent of the subordination of women in the biblical materials. But whereas much traditional interpretation sanctioned this picture, the response of the post-Christian feminist is to say that the biblical text must be rejected, as the irredeemable product of a 'patriarchal' culture, and with it any notion of scriptural authority in the traditional sense.

However, there is (in spite of all) much in the Old Testament that is more positive with regard to women than either most traditional exegesis or post-Christian feminism has generally acknowledged. Two examples can suffice here. One is the story of Ruth, the Moabite woman who leaves her homeland out of loyalty to her mother-in-law Naomi and settles in Judah, where she becomes the ancestress of David. The other is the remarkable motif of the personification of the divine Wisdom as a woman in Proverbs chapter eight. Indeed, one of the major contributions of what we might call 'mainstream' feminist exegesis of the Bible has been to demonstrate this more positive side. A good example of the presentation of positive themes is Phyllis Trible's *God and the Rhetoric of Sexuality*, in which texts ranging from Genesis chapter one to the Song of Songs are explored from a feminist perspective.[4] This position certainly acknowledges the so-called 'patriarchy' of much of the biblical witness, but it wrestles with the question of how this may be related to those parts of the text which are more positive about women. Because such 'mainstream' feminist writers attribute some distinctive authority to the Bible (unlike post-Christian feminists), they engage in an important way with issues of change and continuity within the Christian tradition and with questions relating to the authority of Scripture.[5]

Among the important questions of interpretation highlighted by the work of these feminist critics are the following: How are we to respond to the fact that both 'positive' and 'negative' themes concerning women are to be found side-by-side in the Bible? Should we give greater weight to one or the other, and, if so, on what grounds?

One response is the attempt to make the most of the 'positive' themes concerning women and the feminine in the biblical tradition, thereby counteracting the 'negative' bias of much traditional interpretation. Katharine Doob Sakenfeld identifies two aspects of such an approach. One involves giving renewed emphasis to texts in which women play a prominent, positive role; a notable example would be the stories about Deborah, the deliverer of Israel, recounted in Judges chapters four and five. The second aspect involves the positive reinterpretation of texts, finding 'positive' themes in material which has traditionally been thought to present a 'negative' view of women. An example of the latter would be the attempt of some critics to emphasise the co-responsibility of woman with man in the Eden narrative as a positive theme.[6]

This approach, which we might call 'maximising the positive', has many attractions; it is certainly illuminating to be helped to read with new eyes a narrative such as that of Moses' infancy in Exodus chapters one and two, where we discover the important role played by women as the agents of God's saving activity.[7] However, there are also reasons to be cautious here, two of which we shall briefly examine.

First, there is the danger of attempting to reclaim too much, trying to redeem the irredeemable. Occasionally, one feels that eisegesis rather than exegesis is at work; this criticism is certainly made by some of those who study the place of women in the biblical world from a more strictly historical viewpoint.[8] Moreover, one detects in some feminist exegesis a certain lack of clarity with regard to what is being claimed. At times, it is not quite clear whether the reader is being offered a historical-critical judgment about the original meaning of the text or a free reading for our own day, which does not necessarily claim to tally with the original meaning; indeed, some feminist critics appear to slide between the two.[9] We must beware of being simplistic in our criticism here, for the relationship between exegesis of an ancient text and its appropriation in a modern situation is, of course, always a complex one. Nevertheless, more consistent clarity about what is being claimed by feminist exegetes would undoubtedly help others weigh the value of their contribution.

Second, even when it is employed appropriately, the approach which we have dubbed 'maximising the positive' has obvious limitations. For there will inevitably remain texts for which no reinterpretation seems possible, a significant residue of what some have called 'irredeemably sexist material'. Integrity and honesty demand that such 'negative' texts be acknowledged for what they are. But how then are we to deal with them?

The approach of Phyllis Trible in her book *Texts of Terror* is a sophisticated attempt to grapple with this very question.[10] She reviews four particularly gruesome narratives. The first is the story of Hagar, the Egyptian maid who bears Abraham's son Ishmael but becomes the innocent victim of rejection (Genesis 16.1–16; 21.9–21). The next is the account of the rape of Tamar, princess of Judah, by her brother Amnon (2 Samuel 13.1–22). Trible's third text is the harrowing tale of the betrayal, rape and dismemberment of an unnamed concubine from Bethlehem (Judges 19.1–30). And then, finally, there is the story of the sacrifice of Jephthah's daughter, in fulfilment of the father's foolish vow (Judges 11.29–40). Trible is not concerned to rehabilitate her 'texts of terror', in the sense of demonstrating that they are positive after all. On the contrary, she presents them in all their darkness, calling the reader to identify with biblical women both in their oppression and in their struggle for freedom. These four texts are themselves undeniably 'negative', and yet Trible enables an engagement with these biblical narratives which is both profound and challenging.

We have mentioned the attempt to discern and highlight more 'positive' themes. We have also seen that even 'negative' passages can, in a sense, be used positively. But given that both 'negative' and 'positive' themes are to be found, how are they to be related? Can we find any criteria which might help us to order these diverse biblical materials?

The approach of Rosemary Radford Ruether attempts to address this question by looking beyond those texts which speak explicitly of women. She claims to discern in the Bible a more general theological perspective which is the key to the whole. She finds this in what she calls 'Prophetic Principles'. These, she says, 'imply a rejection of . . . every use of God to justify social domination and subjection'. [11] Within the Old Testament, these principles are found in, for example, the Exodus tradition and the Classical Prophets. This strand of the biblical witness is given normative status – and all biblical 'sexism' (to use Ruether's word) is subordinated to its critique. Whilst many passages make no reference to the situation of women, they give a scriptural charter for the liberation of women in our own day. Consciousness of oppression is contextual, Ruether stresses, and the appropriate response in the modern context is to make explicit the critique of sexism which is implicit in the 'Prophetic Principles' of the Old Testament.

This approach is, in many ways, attractive. But why should we elevate these 'Prophetic Principles' to normative status? The Old Testament presents us with a very 'mixed bag' of materials on most issues of major concern, including those of power and justice. There are, of course, legitimate debates about what is central and what is marginal, but it is by no means clear on what grounds 'Prophetic Principles' could conclusively be shown to be normative in the Old Testament. [12] There are indeed many texts which might be used to support feminist concerns (and these might well include some which contain no explicit reference to women), but there are clearly also many other texts which point in a different direction. Some feminist critics weaken their case by failing adequately to address this question of the criteria upon which selection is to be made and emphasis given. [13]

This is ultimately, of course, an issue of authority. The Christian may wish at this point to bring in the New Testament and ask whether it can yield the key to our problem. We have, after all, been using the term Old Testament (rather than Hebrew Bible), which implies a Christian theological context. Cannot the New Testament show us what should be the normative, authoritative emphasis within the diverse materials of the Old? But here we face the difficulty that the diversity of the New Testament witness on the place of women and the feminine is comparably complex to that of the Old Testament. How, for example, are we to reconcile Jesus' apparently positive attitude towards women with the so-called subordinationist texts in Paul, both of course much debated? No more than the Old Testament does the New Testament, in its own right, give us unequivocal grounds for attributing greater authority to one emphasis rather than another.[14]

One way forward seems to lie in broadening the scope of our inquiry still further. Our principles of discrimination can be drawn only in part from within the Bible; we have to go outside Scripture too. Ruether is, in practice, quite evidently drawing on a whole range of extra-biblical considerations when she chooses to give primacy to her 'Prophetic Principles'.[15] And this is surely nothing new; throughout the centuries, whatever interpreters have *claimed* they were doing, they have in fact operated with their own 'canon' within the biblical canon, conditioned by their own theological, confessional and ideological perspectives.[16] Today we see the range of factors involved to be broad indeed (certainly including philosophical, sociological, political and psychological factors). Robert Morgan has reminded us recently just how multi-faceted is this task of biblical interpretation.[17] It is important that we should acknowledge that we are all engaged in a broadly-based theological endeavour such as this when we read Scripture. Such a recognition will compel us to reflect self-critically upon this task and upon the difficult question of how we can appropriately express the authority of the Bible within such a process. Moreover, we shall find ourselves forced to think hard about a host of closely-related questions, concerning revelation and natural theology, change and continuity within a religious tradition, the development of doctrine and the inspiration of the Holy Spirit, issues of objectivity and subjectivity, committed reading and detachment, and the importance of the context of interpretation. In short, we shall be required to think theologically.

Feminist exegesis not only poses an important challenge to many of our assumptions about the Bible and about ourselves with regard to the place of women and the feminine; it also highlights, as we have seen, many issues which are central to all interpretation of the Bible. If we have raised several critical questions concerning the method of feminist exegesis, this is in the recognition that these issues are being addressed by a number of feminist critics themselves, and also that these methodological observations have a bearing upon most other forms of biblical interpretation too.

In closing, we shall summarise the main general issues of method which have been highlighted.

1. It is important to strive for clarity about what is being claimed in biblical interpretation. Above all, we should avoid any tendency to imply in a merely casual or covert way that our reading coincides with the original meaning. If historical-critical judgments *are* offered, they must be defended with exegetical rigour.

2. The diversity of Scripture on most important issues must be acknowledged; where the 'centre' of the biblical witness on any particular theme lies is rarely, if ever, self-evident; as we sift the biblical resources we must reflect self-critically on the criteria upon which selection is made and emphasis given.

3. It is to be acknowledged that, in practice, these criteria are usually drawn from a wide range and that interpretation is always influenced by many extra-biblical factors; that it is indeed shaped, to a significant degree, by the entire context of interpretation. We must strive to express our understanding of the authority of Scripture in such a way as to take seriously the fact that the Bible is but one factor (albeit of foundational importance) in the complex business of finding meaning and identity as Christians in a changing world.

NOTES

1. Elizabeth Cady Stanton, *The Woman's Bible* (London, 1985; first published 1895); cf. Elizabeth Griffin, *In Her Own Right: The Life of Elizabeth Cady Stanton* (Oxford, 1984).
2. Of the wide range of examples which might be cited, we note: Irenaeus, *Against Heresies*, III, 22, 4; Tertullian, *On the Dress of Women*, I, 1, 1–2; Augustine, *Literal Commentary on Genesis*, XI, 42; Ambrose, *On Paradise*, XII, 56.
3. Mary Daly's influential contributions include: *Beyond God the Father* (London, 1985; first published 1973); *Gyn/Ecology* (London, 1984; first

published 1978). Cf. Daphne Hampson, 'The Challenge of Feminism to Christianity', in *Theology* September 1985, pp. 341–50; 'Is There a Place for Feminists in the Christian Church?', in *New Blackfriars* January 1987, pp. 1ff.

4. Phyllis Trible, *God and the Rhetoric of Sexuality* (Philadelphia, 1978).

5. The focus of my concerns in this short essay is with change and development within the *Christian* tradition and its implications for hermeneutics and the authority of Scripture within that tradition. This is in no way to overlook important work being done in this area by those who stand within the Jewish tradition. See, for example, Judith Hauptman, 'Images of Women in the Talmud', in Rosemary Radford Ruether (ed.), *Religion and Sexism: Images of Woman in the Jewish and Christian Traditions* (New York, 1974), pp. 184–212.

6. Katharine Doob Sakenfeld, 'Feminist Uses of Biblical Materials', in Letty M. Russell (ed.), *Feminist Interpretation of the Bible* (Oxford, 1985), pp. 55–64.

7. This feature of the narrative is attractively highlighted in Hans-Ruedi Weber, *Experiments with Bible Study* (Geneva, 1981), pp. 67–74.

8. I am grateful for the observations of Léonie Archer here. As an example of her written contribution in this area, see 'The Virgin and the Harlot in the Writings of Formative Judaism', *History Workshop* 24 (1987), pp. 1–16; cf. also Léonie Archer, *Her Price is Beyond Rubies: The Jewish Woman in Graeco-Roman Palestine* (Sheffield, 1990).

9. Such ambiguity is an occasional feature even of Trible's valuable treatment of Genesis chs 2–3: Phyllis Trible, *God and the Rhetoric of Sexuality*, pp. 72–143.

10. Phyllis Trible, *Texts of Terror: Literary-Feminist Readings of Biblical Narratives* (Philadelphia, 1984).

11. Rosemary Radford Ruether, *Sexism and God-Talk: Towards a Feminist Theology* (London, 1983), p. 23; cf. 'Feminism and Patriarchal Religion: Principles of Ideological Critique of the Bible', in the *Journal for the Study of the Old Testament* 22 (1982), pp. 54–66.

12. Among valuable recent treatments of the diversity of the Old Testament, see: Paul D. Hanson, *The Diversity of Scripture: A Theological Interpretation* (Philadelphia, 1982); John Goldingay, *Theological Diversity and the Authority of the Old Testament* (Grand Rapids, Michigan, 1987).

13. When Ruether asserts that the 'prophetic-liberating tradition of Biblical faith . . . can be fairly claimed, on the basis of generally accepted Biblical scholarship, to be the central tradition' she is surely underestimating the problematic nature of this question (Rosemary Radford Ruether, *Sexism and God-Talk*, pp. 23–4).

14. On the New Testament, see Robert Morgan's essay in the present volume.

15. Ruether's formulation of 'Prophetic Principles' would seem to reflect the influence of Marxism, Liberation Theology and secular Feminism, among other factors.
16. Cf. John H. Hayes and Frederick C. Prussner, *Old Testament Theology: Its History and Development* (London, 1985).
17. Robert Morgan (with John Barton), *Biblical Interpretation* (Oxford, 1988).

2

Feminist Theological Interpretation of the New Testament

Robert Morgan

The sub-title of this collection, *Women, Theology and the Christian Tradition*, was intended to invite contributors either to select some historical aspect of that tradition's material concerning women, or to take up the methodological issue of how anyone doing theology, i.e. seeking to understand and communicate Christian faith, should handle this sometimes difficult and embarrassing material. Neither alternative involves actually doing 'feminist theology'. Most of us doubted that we were in a position to do it, but hoped that drawing up some of the relevant material or discussing how it might be used would encourage others better placed and equipped to perform what we agreed to be an important and necessary task. What follows will therefore not venture beyond prolegomena.

Such modesty was appropriate, at least on the part of the male historians, exegetes and theologians involved. If feminist theology were merely the ideological arm of a campaign to bring freedom and justice to women in the Church it might actually be more appropriate for men to take up the burden, and fulfil the law of Christ in love for the neighbour. But without minimising the Christian's commitment to justice, and the place of theology in that struggle, the main contribution of feminist theology should surely be found elsewhere.

Theology involves interpreting the tradition in the light of experience, and vice versa, and the essential contribution of feminist theology to the life of the Christian community is to articulate women's experience and ensure that it receives due weight in understanding and communicating the Christian gospel. An awareness of women's or anyone else's experience of oppression challenges all Christians to do what they can to remove it, but the motivations for such action lie in the gospel itself, as this can be adequately understood by all, and must be argued on that theological basis, not in terms of the historical experience that alerted the Church to the issue. It is a matter of Christian theology as such, not feminist theology in particular. This has a more radical responsibility: to draw out aspects of the gospel and its illumination of human experience which have undoubtedly been submerged by the impoverishment resulting from the massive male domination of Christian institutions and theological production.

Such theology must be done by women, and is one reason why the training of women theologians, and their appointment to positions of leadership in the Christian community, is a matter of some urgency. The famous 'principle of the unripeness of time' usually applicable in church politics (since religion is one thing men and even women do with their conservatism) is no longer applicable here. The gospel has to be heard proclaimed 'in a different voice', to borrow the title of Carol Gilligan's important book, as well as in the different languages of all nations, races and educational levels. In Christ these barriers are overcome, but that means that the gospel can be heard in many idioms, not that differences no longer exist, or can be safely ignored. It is striking that at mammoth meetings of the Society for New Testament Studies, behind whose formidable scholarly batteries stand much practical Christianity and deep theological commitment, there is barely a woman theologian or exegete to be seen. Even more shocking is the lack of much sense of incongruity about this.

The point of an opening disclaimer renouncing any intention of actually engaging in feminist theology is partly lest the title raise false expectations, but partly also to justify paying little attention to what has so far been done in this field, concentrating instead on how to do what ought to be done. We are still witnessing the very early stages of feminist theological interpretations of the New Testament and there is not much clarity about how they might develop. Only one New Testament scholar has so far made a major contribution. It therefore seems best to offer some distinctions and propose some guidelines which can be discussed by all, and to draw on a couple of texts and on the work of Elizabeth Schüssler Fiorenza only to illustrate the points made.

'Feminist theological interpretation' is an ambiguous as well as a clumsy phrase, because it is not clear which of the two adjectives is emphasised, or how they are related to each other. They could even be contradictory, since feminism and theology seem to be more often opposed than in agreement. The overlap implied by the phrase is a small corner of both fields. Feminist interpretation and theological interpretation are different, referring to different codes or frameworks in terms of which a text may be read, and with that in mind the most natural exegesis of the combined phrase is one that makes 'feminist theology' the code or framework in terms of which the New Testament is being read. But that would better be called 'feminist theology's interpretations of the New Testament'. That is still fairly ambiguous, but it is clear where the ambiguities lie: in the phrase 'feminist theology', which may be Christian, non-Christian or post- (i.e. anti-) Christian.

The phrase here chosen to identify our interpretative code, 'feminist theological', contains ambiguities of its own, as well as those it shares with the phrase 'feminist theology'. But these latter can at once be reduced by stating that only Christian theology is under consideration here. That does not dispel the ambiguity, because both 'Christian' and 'theology' are essentially contested concepts, but here too it is possible baldly to state a position: Theology has to do with God who is worshipped, i.e. it is parasitic upon some religion (since these are where God is named and worshipped), and requires an adjective identifying the religious tradition and community to which it belongs, however loosely. Christian theology is not to be confused with philosophical analysis of the concept of God (though it may include that) or with the scientific study of religion, which it also involves.

The distinction, despite overlap, between theology and philosophy of religion has to be underlined because in a European Christian context 'philosophy of religion' meant in effect 'philosophy of the Christian religion' (still the name of a chair in Oxford) and was scarcely distinguishable from Christians' natural theology. The echoes of this now quite distant Christian culture encourage modern theological rationalism. In the eighteenth century this could still express a Christian theology. Today it actually subverts religion by failing to take seriously the character and context of religious discourse. In a secularist and pluralist culture where only religions speak seriously of God, and usually do so on the basis of a claim to revelation, somehow enshrined or witnessed to in their tradition, especially (where applicable) their scriptures, a more 'confessional' style of theology is inescapable. The Christian religion refers to Jesus, its crucified and risen Lord, as the decisive revelation of God; Christian theology unfolds the response to that alleged revelation, and relates the rest of human knowledge and experience to that decisive event.

The boundaries of 'Christian' are admittedly disputed. The reference to a decisive saving revelation of God in Jesus is here taken as the essential criterion, leaving open (for present purposes) the question how it is rightly understood or best expressed. Some reference to Christian community is also essential, and the boundaries even less clear. But the confessional character of theology today, and therefore of theological interpretation, is one of the terms of reference implied by our title.

Restricting these reflections to prolegomena to a Christian feminist theological interpretation of Scripture means setting aside (with respect) Jewish feminist theological interpretation. It is possible for Jewish theologians to interpret the New Testament theologically, i.e. on the assumption that it speaks of God, albeit heretically; but they would not be engaged in scriptural interpretation, because it is not for them Scripture.

The boundaries of Christianity are harder to draw as against 'post-Christian' interpretations of the Bible because these contain some residue of Christianity and are in some cases clearly theological, albeit (to orthodox ears) heretical. For all its frequently aggressive secularism there is also a strong religious element in feminism which is sometimes contained by and sometimes breaks the banks of existing religions. To call 'post-Christian' feminism 'anti-Christian' is brutal but honest. The Christian community engages in healthy inner-theological conflict as disturbing new insights are absorbed, dead branches identified and pruned, and corruptions excised. The theological struggle of feminist Christians for what they consider a better understanding and practice of the gospel is entirely legitimate so long as they themselves remain open to challenge by the gospel at work in the community (often proclaimed by males), and to self-correction as a result of hearing it afresh. But to 'go out from us' (1 John 2.19, cf. 4.1), to leave the (sectarian) community and label oneself 'post-Christian' is (apart from being slightly superior and slightly precious) to risk abandoning the Christian theological task by cutting oneself off from the usual channels of grace and sources of knowledge of God. It substitutes the apostate's undifferentiated war-cry (*Ecrasez l'infâme*) for the reformer's theological zeal. Both responses stem from the same perception of truth, but one is authentically Christian, the other in principle anti-Christian.

Non-Christian interpretations of the Bible are not necessarily anti-religious. The Bible is a public text, available to readers who have no connection with a religious community. Feminists of any religion or none may see propaganda potential in influencing the way such culturally still influential texts as the Bible are read, and so propose feminist readings of this material. But they will only be theological interpretations of the New Testament if there remains some fundamentally positive relationship to Christianity, however fractured. This does not exclude criticism of some of its statements, as we shall see. But the criticised statements will be recognised as inadequate statements about God who is worshipped, only within the ambience of a worshipping community. When the religious frame of reference is abandoned, theological interpretation withers, because theology is parasitic upon religion. Not even corrupt and out-dated forms of ecclesiastical framework can be abandoned without risk. For Christians, even strategic withdrawals are acts of desperation.

All this attempted clarification of what is meant by 'theological' in our title would be equally relevant to an essay on 'feminist theology's interpretation of the New Testament'. But the phrase 'feminist theological interpretation of the New Testament' is intended to throw the emphasis on the notion of 'theological interpretation' itself, and allow the adjective 'feminist' to qualify that phrase, rather than to have the adjective 'theological' qualifying 'feminist interpretation'. The difference of emphasis is significant for what follows. It means that our starting-point and essential theme is not feminist theology or feminist interpretation, but theological interpretation.

'Feminist interpretation of Scripture' might have brought us to the same starting-point, because the notion of Scripture implies a religious community finding in these writings reference to the God it worships. 'The New Testament' is also a theologically loaded phrase, referring to Christian Scripture. But that can equally now refer to the collection of twenty-seven books which has a place in Western culture, regardless of religious belief. It is therefore necessary to insert the word 'theological' in order to make explicit that it is Christian religious use of the Bible that is under consideration here, not the kind of biblical scholarship or feminist ideology which make no reference to the question of God. Both these are involved here, but as means not ends, means to Christian theology and practice, not the equally legitimate goals of biblical scholarship or feminism.

'Theological' is not the only word in our title that requires some explanation. Equally elusive is the word 'interpretation', which switches the focus away from exclusively exegetical concern with the texts being interpreted, and includes the other end of the interpretative act – the persons engaged in it. This 'modern end' is important because interpreters have their own aims and interests which only partly coincide with those of the biblical authors, and because these may influence how individual texts are read.

It is normal for biblical scholars to see their task as avoiding such distortions and explaining what the text is actually saying, i.e. what the linguistic conventions meant when it was written, not what some modern reader would like to think it means. This is correct, and linguistic and historical exegesis important. But when we ask why it is important, we find it hard to claim that it is all-important. Responsible exegesis is important because readers generally want to know what the text has to say. That is particularly clear when the Bible is read by Christians, because they presuppose it has something vital to teach them about God and the world, something which they need to hear. A theory of meaning that emphasises the creativity of interpreters at the expense of the content of the texts themselves is in principle undesirable even if in practice unavoidable. A second, more pragmatic argument for stable meanings, and against textual indeterminacy, also applies to scriptural interpretation. Textual exegesis of some, e.g. legal, texts is important because the community using them needs some shared understanding of their meaning. The grammatical meaning provides some basis for this.

Both these arguments for linguistic and historical exegesis appeal to the interests of the modern readers. Exegesis is not valuable purely for its own sake, but the readers, on whose account it is important, may have a variety of interests in the text, not all of which require historical exegesis, and some of which may imply a higher priority than strict exegesis. Depending on how a text is used, other factors may affect how it is understood. To take the legal example again: precedent is sometimes important, and an authoritative ruling may determine how a statute is understood within a civil community. The Bible seems different, because Christians expect to learn something from their Scripture; it is not for them (essentially) a law-book, even though it is often treated as such. But Christians do have other interests and the exegesis of particular texts in such a diverse collection of material poses problems. They look for a unity in their canon, and they need to assume that it is true and reliable – factual errors and moral inadequacies are a problem. Above all they need some kind of correspondence between their Scriptures and their own religious system of belief, and this has been a problem from the beginning for a movement whose Scriptures were written by authors and edited in a community that had never heard of Jesus.

As that implies, tension between what the scriptural text is plainly saying, and what religious readers take it to mean, is not new. Some of the ways in which theologians have handled and still handle this difficulty will be found applicable in feminist theological interpretation of the New Testament. But before these are considered the shape of the problem itself needs to be clarified.

It is a problem liable to confront any ideologically motivated interpretation of a very diverse collection of texts which is regarded by the interpreters as an authoritative source of their ideology (using that word in its non-pejorative sense). Marxists have problems with some of the things Marx said, and Freudians with some of their master's comments – both, significantly, in the light of more recently acknowledged feminist insights. In the interpretation of Scripture it is essentially a problem of theological interpretation. Christians are guided in their understanding of the gospel by an authoritative Scripture, and therefore have an interest in what the scripture actually says. Exegesis is therefore important. But even though it is typically individual passages which make an impact, Christians are never dependent on individual texts in isolation. They are dependent on their Scripture as a whole, which contains a very large collection of texts. But if they never see individual texts in isolation, neither do they in practice see Scripture 'as a whole', in isolation. They always see it already interpreted, and interpreted in terms of their own religious system. This kaleidoscope of texts is open to an infinite number of possible combinations, some of which yield Christian interpretations of the whole. These provide the lens through which, or framework in terms of which, they read all the individual parts of the bible.

Our problem is that of the relationship between the Christian framework and the individual texts, some of which in isolation may say things that contradict the framework. The reason this is a problem is that the framework in some sense depends on the individual texts, so it is impossible to reject many of these without eroding the framework, and weakening the actual criterion by which they are rejected. The problem seems most acute to Protestants because they insist on a very close relationship between their Christian framework and Scripture, though even they do not identify their framework with Scripture. Even fundamentalists work with a framework which has been shaped to fit a certain way of reading Scripture. The major dispute between theological interpreters is between those who think that every text must be fitted to their Christian framework (biblicists) and those who feel free to reject particular texts which conflict with this. The latter sub-divide between those who try to limit the damage of erosion done to their scriptural source (critical Protestants) and those who do not (liberals).

There is always a two-way traffic between the interpreter's theological framework and the historical exegesis of particular texts. The latter must be done as conscientiously as possible and be allowed to challenge, perhaps even alter, the framework which guides Christians' engagement with particular passages and their combinations of these with other passages. Theologians have to maintain a delicate balance, respecting what a particular text is saying, but also seeking to relate it to the larger system they are trying to clarify and communicate. Most Christians' theological framework is sufficiently supple to accommodate most of the New Testament without difficulty, but occasionally an issue arises, such as feminism and anti-Semitism in the West today, or totalitarianism, racialism, and the nuclear threat, which makes certain texts suddenly appear highly problematic to theologically responsible Christians.

Occasionally Christians may be persuaded by a particular text, or rather a particular understanding of a text, to revise their understanding of the gospel and what this requires of them. More usually their prior understanding of Christianity will outweigh any difficult text.[1] The theological importance of an exegesis which sets aside the larger Christian framework and sees each text in its original context is that this can sharpen the Church's listening to, and being challenged by, its Scripture. It can dismiss some interpretations as implausible, and help keep theology a matter of rational argument. But reinforcing the witness of individual texts and keeping theology responsibly self-critical does not (or should not) negate the interpreters' attempts to relate Scripture to their understanding of the gospel. It makes their task more difficult, but not impossible. Those who abandon the task as impossible, and stop trying to ground their Christianity in the Bible, may unintentionally lead the church away from the gospel. On the other hand, identifying the gospel with the letter of Scripture leads to impossible contradictions and even to sub-Christian conclusions. A critical middle way is needed, giving Scripture due weight but allowing us to question what it is saying.

That is what critical theological interpretation aims to provide, and since feminist theological interpretation is a form of this, the problems and procedures will be the same. The first task is to describe the interpretative framework, the second to allow this (as well as exegesis, with its alternative, historical framework) to influence our engagement with particular texts.

'Feminist-theological' implies a relationship between two different frameworks of systems or belief and values: Christianity and feminism. Reasons have been given for making Christianity the overarching framework here, while expecting the feminist case to influence this. What changes in Christian practice and belief (if any) the feminist movement should stimulate is a theological question about the essential nature and future shape of Christianity. This is debated and tested within the Christian community, partly through its attending to its Scripture and tradition, partly through its relating these to its on-going and developing experience, which includes the growth of a feminist consciousness inside and outside the Church. The converse question, how Christian insights might influence women's understanding of their experience, is better left for women theologians to discuss.

The two-way traffic in which theological frameworks and the exegesis of individual texts relate and sometimes collide, is part of the process through which the impact of feminism on traditional understandings of the gospel take place. But this interaction presupposes some preliminary definition of the framework, to which we now turn.

Christians' understanding of Christianity, i.e. their theological frameworks, are always provisional, open to new insights. On the other hand Christianity does have some defining characteristics without which a position can scarcely be deemed Christian at all. The claim that God, known in the Bible and Church, is decisively revealed in Jesus, is definitive. To move 'beyond' these parameters (as anyone must who thinks them incompatible with the truth about human existence) is to part company with Christianity. But they are fairly wide parameters and have in the past proved sufficiently flexible to absorb new knowledge and moral insight. Their weakness has been that they are too flexible to preserve the identity of a religious community, and have had to be reinforced by further doctrinal clarification and institutional supports. But for our purposes of theological exploration the looseness and flexibility of this christological criterion is an advantage. The bottom line for Christians is the revelation of God in Jesus, but the whole range of modern knowledge and experience may be drawn into clarifying that, including whatever is right and true in feminism, which itself is a matter of exploration and experience, undertaken in a Christian context of listening attentively to Scripture. In this process some aspects of the Christian tradition and also some aspects of contemporary feminism may be confirmed, and other aspects of both criticised, in the light of the gospel as this is heard afresh when the tradition and the experience of the two movements are brought together.

If Christianity can be summed up in a sentence to identify the overarching framework, so can the movement which is challenging or claiming a voice in it. Feminism is women's struggle to be themselves, no longer defined in terms of their (subordinate) relationship to men. The demand for justice, especially equality of opportunity, and the keyword 'freedom', are expressions of that aspiration, and many Christians would say that this much at least corresponds to the good news of God that Jesus embodies.

But when Christians and other humanists say what they think is involved in humans being their true selves, conflicting visions emerge. Even such shared ideals as freedom and justice look different in the context of different world-views. All of us are opposed to human bondage, but different remedies imply different accounts of reality and different assessments of the human predicament. Talk of conversion, reconciliation and a relationship to God, implies a more pessimistic view of present realities and a more optimistic view of human possibilities than secular humanism can admit. Both sides value human freedom, but a freedom defined as the willing service of God in the Spirit looks very different from Enlightenment autonomy. Even justice, where Christianity has absorbed more of the Greek spirit, is far more than distributive justice if the compassionate God is our final norm.

The differences, however, should not be overstated. The Enlightenment owed much to Christian humanism, and modern Christianity has accepted as much of the rationalist critique as seemed justified. By altering some of its social and doctrinal stances it has both preserved the credibility of its claims and ensured that the remaining differences express a genuine alternative to the easy optimism of the age of reason and the bleak pessimism which follows, not a series of fossils from now discredited world-views. In this far from complete theological process, the encounter with feminism is currently the most important arena for Western Christianity.

As a modern emancipatory movement the most obvious roots of feminism lie in the European Enlightenment. They have not (as yet) produced an independent religious, moral or political system. Feminism has developed within the larger existing systems of modern Western humanism and has usually expressed its positive values through criticism of existing social structures and ideologies. Christianity and Judaism, even Marxism and psycho-analysis, have been subject to insider and outsider feminist criticism, but always piecemeal. They have not (as yet, anyway) been challenged by an alternative feminist view of the world. The movement is therefore still best defined in terms of what it opposes, namely the oppression of women and denials of their full humanity. The visions of humanity which it affirms are developments of the particular traditions in which it works as a leaven. When systematically unfolded the ideals of Christian feminists and Marxist feminists vary and even conflict. What unites them all is their opposition to a whole area in which all the different humanistic traditions of the West fall short of their own ideals.

If this is correct, it vindicates the decision to make Christianity our overarching framework, and also suggests a political dimension to the task of feminist theological interpretation. This interprets Scripture in ways which will persuade other Christians to repudiate and resist oppression. Christians say that the legitimate aspirations of feminism are better expressed within the (corrected) Christian system than elsewhere, and work to make that religious ideal a social reality.

But that leaves unanswered the crucial question of which aspirations are legitimate. There is theological disagreement here, which the Christian community seeks to resolve by listening to Scripture and reflecting on its corporate and personal experience, much of which it shares with the wider non-Christian world.

The critical area is evidently the relation between the sexes, especially within marriage, which Christianity values highly, and has some firm views on. The question is whether women's subordination is one of these firm views, as some biblical texts suggest.

Before looking at any of these texts, theologians need to be aware of their own Christian framework and the ways in which it may be modified by the texts. Any Christian framework or understanding of the gospel depends heavily on Scripture and may be influenced by the witness of individual texts. It is shaped by a long history of tradition and experience in which the Church's listening to Scripture has played a major role, but not the only role. The texts are filtered through our understanding of the gospel, even though in the process they might alter it. We approach the texts from where and what we are, our beliefs and attitudes shaped by a variety of factors. We can hold much of this in suspense, in order to hear what a text or another person is saying, but in some contexts it is important not to deny our preconceptions and responses. Some forms of address, including religious speech and other invitations to share a life, such as declarations of love, or challenges to one's value system, are directed at us so personally that it is important not to relegate them to the level of interesting historical information, even if the disciplines of historical method are necessary to decode them.

The Bible does not have to be read in this highly charged manner, and Christians do not usually read or hear most of the Bible as personal address. It is enough to recognise that a passage might become such. But that is the point at which it has most religious authority. The Bible contains historical information and doctrinal data relevant to its foundational role in Christianity, but a text is most powerfully authoritative for a Christian at the moments when it is felt actually to mediate divine revelation. There are different layers to the Christian use of the Bible. Both historical information and symbolic vocabulary are important in several different ways. But an individual text has supreme authority for an individual Christian only in those critical moments in which insight dawns and God is acknowledged, an event in which the believer stands himself or herself exposed. But they can adduce considerations which may help others to share their own understanding of the gospel and its relation to the text under consideration. What the text says is then taken up into the more personal question of what it says to me. That is subject to the necessary exegetical controls, but it is mainly influenced by what the interpreter brings to the text. This means that in approaching a text which seems to have some bearing on an issue (e.g. subordination within marriage or equality of the sexes), general reflections on both the question at issue and the gospel itself have priority, and may even override individual texts. Our brief discussion of that critical area must start with such general reflections.

Some differentiation of roles seems inescapable within marriage, and appropriate elsewhere, on account of biology. But neither child-bearing nor (typically) a degree of physical weakness implies inferiority, or even subordination, since status cannot for Christians be based on physical power. Partnership is self-evidently more appropriate in describing Christian understandings of marriage than male (or female) domination. But is it a partnership of equals, and what might that mean?

Equality is an Enlightenment ideal with less obvious Christian antecedents than freedom or justice. Like toleration, it might be an area where traditional religion can thank modernity for highlighting features present in its own tradition, and for pointing it towards authentic developments of that tradition. Equality of opportunity is implied by justice and is uncontroversial. Equality before God is basic Christian belief. Structures of domination can easily be shown to be contrary to the Christian profession. But hierarchical structures, including the subordination of women (at least within marriage), are not incompatible with notions of partnership and are strongly written into the Christian tradition.

This seems to be a point where some Christians' experience of marriage in the present-day West compels them to challenge earlier views and to claim that modern assumptions about equality of the sexes represent a moral advance. They cannot seriously entertain the notion that wives are junior partners, or subject in a one-sided way to their husbands. They must therefore suppose that biblical passages enjoining subordination are simply reflecting social situations that no longer obtain. They may admit that the tradition contains a wealth of wisdom and experience, and should not be set aside lightly. But any attempt to recommend patriarchy simply on appeal to certain texts will be suspected of legitimating one's own interests or preferences.

However, a simple appeal to experience is as unsatisfactory here as a simple appeal to biblical texts. Neither is a Christian theological argument unless it is based on an understanding of what Christianity is, based as that is on both tradition (including Scripture) and experience. Even if we make most of our provisional theological judgments intuitively it is necessary then to argue a case for their being true to the gospel. This includes appealing to the tradition and accounting for those parts of it which support the opposite viewpoint. That is the spade-work of theological interpretation. The adjective 'feminist' simply specifies a particular area which developments in Western society and culture have placed high on our theological agenda. Theological interpretation (feminist, other liberationist, or quite different attempts to develop the tradition in the light of new Christian experience of living the gospel) can be directed at any part of the ever-expanding tradition. That is why 'church history' as well as biblical studies can be a theological discipline. But clearly Scripture is in principle the most authoritative and normative part of the tradition, and in practice the most read or heard. Since Christians understand their experience partly in terms of these texts (or some of them), it is particularly important that they be heard in appropriate ways, and misleading passages challenged in the light of the gospel.

The less our experience is comparable to that of our ancestors, the less direct guidance Scripture is likely to provide, and the more likely its models are to be misleading. That is one reason for theological interpretation preferring theological argument about individual passages to the 'women's history' approach to the New Testament suggested by the hegemony of historical study in modern biblical scholarship. It can also be argued that the ways in which Paul's epistles are authoritative for subsequent Christianity do not imply that first-century church history is authoritative. It is Paul's symbol system which has become normative, and this can be (and usually is) assimilated by Christians who do not know much biblical criticism. Christ crucified and risen, as the decisive moment in which God was reconciling the world, or God's saving righteousness having been and being revealed, and this constituting a new covenant and community into which believers are baptised, receive his Spirit, share his risen life, and look for his coming glory – these are not necessarily matters for historical criticism. Historical study can throw some light on the background of these symbols and so nourish our reflection on them. It can also help justify our theological criticism of some details. But its main contribution to theology is at the level of exegesis, which benefits from historical understanding, rather than in New Testament theology or symbolics, which is the Church's primary interest in these texts.

Since, however, in practice one of the ways in which Scripture makes its impact is through its supposed historical models, 'feminist historical reconstructions' of Israel and Christian origins have pragmatic value. But they risk reinforcing a theologically unsatisfactory way of reading Scripture. The most theologically valuable parts of Elizabeth Schüssler Fiorenza's important book [2] are not (I suggest) her methodological arguments or her larger historical proposals, but her engagement with particular texts. Such helpful phrases as 'partnership of equals', 'discipleship of equals' and 'the praxis of equal discipleship', which can today function as tests of Christian orthopraxy, are (rightly) as much brought *to* the texts, as deduced from the historical reconstructions.

Because feminist theological interpretation, rightly reflecting some modern experience of living the gospel, is bound to be critical of much of the tradition, it is worth sketching some of the ways in which such 'critical theological interpretation' (*Sachkritik*) has been done without reference to new feminist insights. It is my contention that the same procedures are relevant to listening for the gospel in Scripture, in the light of contemporary feminist sensibility.

The main problem posed by the Bible for Christian theology has always been how to make Christian sense of passages which seem plainly sub-Christian. One solution is to adopt an alternative exegesis, which is less offensive. Thus the 'little ones' to be 'dashed against the rock' in Psalm 137 are referred by Augustine to the individual's own sins, which have to be rooted out, not to Babylonian toddlers. This imposes a genuine Christian meaning on a text whose true meaning is sub-Christian. But allegorical exegesis has run into problems of plausibility in a more historically conscious age, though at the personal devotional level, where no theological (i.e. public) argument is being built, it is widely accepted as a legitimate device for stirring the religious imagination. It never was 'hard' enough to support a theological argument, as Augustine and Aquinas recognised,[3] but it provided a way out of a difficulty which arose from the way scriptural authority and inspiration were once understood. Today we accept that the production of the Bible by fallible human authors and editors involves various imperfections, and explain moral imperfections and other errors in that way, even though this reduces the authority of Scripture and weakens its impact.

The point here (contrary to Origen) is that all Scripture has a literal meaning, but it does not all have a Christian theological meaning. Theological discernment includes recognising where a passage does not apply to ourselves, and also *when* it does not, since some passages can lie dormant for generations and then burst into theological relevance, as Galatians 3.28 has recently done. While admitting that not all biblical texts are likely to illuminate contemporary Christian experience, and insisting that to demand this is to misunderstand the nature of the gospel and the work of the Spirit, we may nevertheless add that it is wise for theological interpreters to look for such illumination, because that is how reflection on biblical texts activates theological reflection and motivates Christian responses. Possessing a 'Scripture' means keeping these texts on the theological agenda, even though certain problems then remain prominent and procedures for handling them are necessary. Occasional difficulties about the content of Scripture keep interpreters awake, and Origen thought this providential.

Limiting the damage done by sub-Christian texts is sometimes a matter of passing them over as not applicable. But where they are appealed to in support of what we think perversions of the gospel, more drastic action is needed. This can be positive or negative.

It is sometimes possible to neutralise dangerous texts by suggesting a less offensive but equally plausible alternative exegesis. That sounds corrupt, and would be if it were a matter of evading what the text is saying. But sometimes it is simply impossible to be sure about that, and one exegesis looks as good as another. The price of accepting this is again a reduction in the text's power to sustain an argument. But again, that is only one, relatively rare, function of Scripture. More usually Scripture works for us by informing us, or else sparking insights in a process where the interpreters themselves bring something to the production of meaning. Even faulty exegesis can (happily) do this, though it must be abandoned when (if) it is recognised to be faulty.

An example of this choosing the better theology is Fiorenza's explanation of 'on account of the angels' at 1 Corinthians 11.10: 'Since the angels are present in the pneumatic worship service of a community that speaks "the tongues of angels", women should not worship as cultically unclean persons by letting their hair down but should pin it up as a sign both of their spiritual power and of their control over their heads' (p. 228). Nobody knows for sure what the phrase means, and Fiorenza is justified in choosing a plausible suggestion which happens to be more positive about women in church than the idea of a Genesis 6 echo (which may possibly reflect some male exegetes' unconscious desires). Women have spiritual power, not just sex-appeal. Not surprisingly, this route of choosing the least offensive plausible exegesis is mostly taken by conservative Protestants who wish to maximise the relevance and authority of Scripture. Liberals may even prefer the exegesis that is more difficult for theology, as part of their short-sighted campaign to reduce this dependence of the Church on Scripture.

Theological interpretation generally seeks to relate individual texts to their original historical frame of reference and to the interpreter's own theological framework. The theological difficulty of some texts can be reduced by careful attention to their historical context. The situation and context may extenuate an offensive remark or reveal that the author's concern was not that of the interpreter. Paul is not promulgating a dogma of women's subordination in 1 Corinthians 11.2–16. He takes it for granted, but does not argue it in terms of the gospel itself. Conversely, the theological fruitfulness of other texts is reduced by a better exegetical understanding. Job 19.25 cannot be used as an argument for the resurrection of Jesus, though it can still be read by Christians (with Handel) as an evocative pointer to that. Modern exegetical methods have significantly advanced the Church's on-going reflection on its Scripture, but this has necessitated a more precise account of the different ways in which Scripture can be used.

One complicating result of modern history of traditions research is that we see some texts as multi-layered. This greatly increases the exegetical possibilities, because we can sometimes ask what a text meant to its final editor(s), and what at earlier stages of the tradition; including, in the case of the Gospels, what some sayings meant to the historical Jesus. Since this is usually rather speculative, it again fails to carry much weight in argument. But there is something artificial about B.S. Childs' suggestion that only the final canonical level has theological authority. Jesus has more authority than Matthew, though (arguably) Matthew and Luke more than their hypothetical source Q. The potential contained in history of traditions research for criticising a biblical text in the (half-)light of earlier forms of a tradition is fruitfully illustrated by Fiorenza (pp. 143–6). Luke's redactional addition of 'wife' to the list of relations a disciple might have to leave introduces an androcentric bias into Jesus' saying (compare Luke 14.26 and 18.29b with Mark 10.29b). Again, *behind* Mark 10.2–9 and 12.18–27, Fiorenza argues, Jesus in effect criticised patriarchal marriage. She thinks the point of 12.25 is abolition not of sexual differentiation in heaven but of the patriarchy sustained by levirate marriage.

These examples are not all equally persuasive, and feminist or any other theological interpretation is a matter of using rational arguments to persuade others to read an authoritative text one way rather than another. These examples all involved an element of rationally justified criticism of the text as it stands. They have therefore prepared us for the most drastic way of dealing with texts which seem sub-Christian: simply to reject them as incompatible with one's understanding of the gospel. Interpreters here allow their own rational judgment, moral sense, and understanding of the gospel, informed as this is (in part) by Scripture itself, to provide the criterion by which a particular text is judged, and judged negatively.

Only a biblicist who identifies the gospel with Scripture, or asserts the infallibility of Scripture, can forbid this in principle. But others are rightly wary of cutting off the branch they are standing on, or killing the plant in pruning it, or disposing of a valuable branch. Too easy a rejection of the witness of a text loses its capacity to challenge one's (always provisional) understanding of the gospel. But there is no contradiction in both appealing to Scripture as a whole and yet challenging particular passages. To those who would like to see Matthew 27.25 expunged or Psalm 137.8–9 etc. placed in brackets, the warning of Revelation 21.29 against excisions is germane. But theological criticism is not surgery. The offending texts continue to be heard and questioned. But reasons are given for suggesting that they are wrong, and to be discounted by Christians. The interpreter's theological convictions here outweigh the individual text. How often this can happen without doing unacceptable damage to the authority of Scripture is a further question.

The theological criticism of individual texts, here defended in principle, offers a middle way between biblicism and the liberal tendency to give contemporary secular experience decisive weight as against Scripture and tradition. That perennial confrontation between conservative and liberal theology has surfaced again in the distinction between 'biblical feminists' (mainly Evangelicals),[4] and 'liberal Christian feminists'.[5] The middle way is both evangelical and critical. It reflects Barth's *Sachexegese* (exegesis concerned with the theological content), as corrected by Bultmann to include *Sachkritik* (criticising individual texts in the light of that same theological content). It emphasises the Christian dependence on Scripture, but insists that Christ, not Scripture as such, is the decisive revelation of God, and that contemporary experience plays an important role in our apprehension of Christ and the Spirit in Scripture. Some Evangelical theology seems to be moving in this direction, while still retaining a strongly biblical shape to its framework.[6] Other Christians travel more lightly, maintaining an orthodox (incarnational) framework, but willing to consign more of the tradition to the history books.

Theological interpretation is best done by studying individual texts because these are what make a direct impact, not the (more or less helpful) constructions of historians and biblical theologians. Exegetical study clarifies the witness of each text, but the relationship to the interpreter's framework is decisive. Here, as in moral theology, 'conscience is always to be followed'. Unless wrestling with a difficult text actually changes our understanding of the gospel (which is very rare) this prior understanding will carry most weight. In our second example a problem text has in the last resort to be overruled. But theological interpretation, the context in which the impact of feminism on Christianity is here being set, also underlines passages which seem to offer positive support. In both cases the historical and exegetical debate about what a text might have meant to the writer is taken up into theological reflection about how it is best to be understood today.

'There is neither Jew nor Greek, there is not slave nor free person, there is not male and female; for you are all one person in Christ Jesus.' Galatians 3.28 demands to be given considerable weight because in context it looks like a doctrinal statement concerning the very nature of Christianity. But the question of its possible meaning for Paul, and for modern interpreters, is complex, involving exegetical arguments and even a theory of religion, because what Paul meant by 'in Christ' can scarcely be articulated without one. If the exegetical debate is inconclusive, this does not matter. Theological interpreters can live with exegetical uncertainty. The debate helps them look at the text from several angles, increasing the possibility that connections with their own understanding of the gospel may crystallise, and the text thus nudge them in a Christian direction, maybe even supporting action which Paul himself did not take.

Paul's theological language is today perhaps best understood in the context of a theory of religion as a system of symbols.[7] The critical question for the modern Christian reader is how far the symbolic language of the gospel contained in Scripture should be shaping social realities today. Some think it only meaningful when it is changing the world. At the other extreme it is possible to confine it to the believer's personal relationship to God, without revolutionary, though not without conservative, social consequences. Paul is clear that there is a strong relationship between at least some of his symbolic or theological language and the social realities of the community. The whole point of his epistle is to persuade his hearers to draw practical conclusions from his theological argument about Torah no longer applying in the new creation in Christ, or new age of faith and the Spirit. 'In Christ' such differences as Jew–Gentile, slave–free, male–female, do not exist, whatever the situation in the Roman empire. And his argument is that the empirical church should correspond at the social level to the symbolic or theological reality, not to the empirical realities of the world outside Christ – at least so far as the then current issue was concerned.

But Paul draws no such radical conclusions from his parallel symbolic statement that in Christ there is no 'male and female', and what he writes in 1 Corinthians suggests some ambivalence about this. He does draw some conclusions elsewhere from the abolition at the symbolic level of slave-free, though not the radical conclusions which most Christians now see implied by it. That implication of the Christian gospel only became self-evident when the time was ripe, and even then at first only to a minority – who set out to persuade others. To many Christians today it is equally clear that Paul's repudiation of social, racial and gender distinctions at the symbolic level must have social consequences also with respect to gender. It is not possible to *deduce* this from Scripture. Being led by the Spirit in listening to Scripture is less mechanical or logical than that. Inspiration involves imagination as much as reason.

Neither is it possible to infer what the consequences should be. These require further theological discussion, stimulated by exegesis of the scriptural tradition as well as by contemporary experience. But the way Paul came to his conclusion about Gentiles is instructive for contemporary Christians thinking about a different, though seemingly parallel issue.

Paul knows already that Gentiles can be Christians without being circumcised or observing the food laws. He has seen it done, and this reality has found symbolic expression in his new theological framework. But he has to persuade others, and that requires rational theological argument from tradition (especially Scripture) and experience. His opponents have a strong case based on tradition, i.e. Scripture. The law of Moses was, after all, God-given, and Jesus the Jewish Messiah. Gentiles were now coming in as prophesied, but presumably they must be circumcised. Even Abraham, having believed, went on to be circumcised.

Against this, Paul knows he is right, and that to accede to his opponents' demands would be to surrender the freedom of life in the Spirit, which the gospel of God in Jesus had established. But he needs a strong argument, rooted in the nature of the gospel, and providing an alternative reading of the tradition. He starts from his understanding of the gospel and will not allow Scripture or tradition to override that (unless persuaded he is wrong), but he still needs the tradition, without which his gospel can be neither expressed nor believed. Religious talk of God generally depends on a previously existing tradition. It is therefore necessary to interpret the tradition afresh in the light of his understanding of the gospel.

Paul's argument from Scripture looks weak (or unintelligible) to anyone not already persuaded, and familiar with rabbinic rules of exegesis. But what seems to the modern historically-trained exegete arbitrary is not so distant from how Scripture is usually heard by Christians: isolated texts can stir a religious response, including sometimes a theological, reflective response. Paul finds support for his conviction in a handful of texts, seized on to construct a fresh reading of the tradition. Genesis 15.6 and Habakkuk 2.4 (and only those two texts) associate right-ness with God with faith, and in them Paul finds support for his understanding of the new relationship to God in Christ. In the course of his discussion he let slip a remark, barely germane to his own argument, which some modern theologians have in a similar way seized on to support what they think is a Spirit-led modern growth in Christian insight: 'There is no male and female'.

They may be right in believing this. The Church has to keep chewing on the text and on other tradition and new experience until the truth of the gospel becomes clear and the right way forward found in a particular dispute such as the terms of admission for Gentiles, divorcees, homosexuals; the abolition of slavery, apartheid, social and ecclesiastical hierarchies; the ordination of members of groups excluded in sections of the Church (in Greece, those who cannot sing; in Rome, married men; in Alexandria and later canon law, eunuchs; in Hippolytus' part of Rome, slaves; in England (at the time of writing) those who have married a divorcee; in Wales, remarried men; in some Christian churches, all women). On none of these or other contemporary questions does Scripture give ready-made answers. It is not a set of instructions rendering superfluous the promise of the Spirit leading disciples into all truth. The Church does not need proof-texts to authorise or prohibit new developments. It dares to experiment and discern which developments in thought and practice are authentic expressions of the gospel, and which are not. A single text may help crystallise new experience into an expression of the gospel, and so give a nudge to new developments.

Galatians 3.28 has for many proved suggestive in this way. It does not provide an unambiguous argument for ordaining women. Paul was not discussing that, and Scripture is not a collection of proof-texts which can by-pass the interpreter's understanding of the gospel. But we may hear it as gospel when we attend to it in the light of our provisional understanding of this. One form of that is experienced when our study of a text takes off into a sermon. Exegetical controls are still important, but the connections then being made are with other things in the interpreter's knowledge and experience, not (essentially) with the historical context. It is not historical learning that speaks of God and makes a biblical interpreter into a theologian, though this can help teach her to be a critical theologian.

The argument about the ordination of women, for example (and it is important to focus theological interpretation on specific issues sometimes), is not settled or even appropriately introduced by appealing to Scripture. The argument is firstly about the enrichment this will bring to the ordained ministry, both in understanding the gospel from a wider experiential base, and in the quality of leadership. It is also about the possible distortion (not merely impoverishment) of such an unrepresentative ministry as a single-sex one appears today. Granted the obvious reason for going ahead, it is secondly necessary to ask 'Why not?' – or 'What prevents?' (cf. Acts 8.36). The arguments from Scripture apparently marshalled against Paul's innovation[8] by opponents whom in retrospect we judge to have been blind to what the Spirit was now doing new, are instructive here. There is thirdly the question of timing, which held William Temple back in 1917. It is related to, but not to be confused with, the question of the truth of the gospel. Paul's guidance on the weak and the strong is relevant here, as is his refusal to allow concessions to weakness to be twisted into denials of the freedom of the gospel (Rom. 14, 1 Cor. 8–10).

In these discussions the Church seeks as always to listen for the

gospel in Scripture. The inconclusiveness of some exegetical
argument can help keep the texts in the forefront of discussion. All
the important points about Galatians 3.28 are plain to any
thoughtful reader of Galatians, but the specialist debates of New
Testament scholars[9] offer a few extra arguments to both sides of
the current controversy, and so hold the text up to on-going scrutiny
while contemporary reflection on the gospel matures.

The discussion aims to throw light on what Paul means by 'no
male and female'. One option is to stress the parallel with the other
phrases, and since sexual, social and racial distinctions still exist
in the real world, to argue that Paul is saying no more than that
all are equal in the sight of God. Against this, he is clearly arguing
for a correspondence between what is the case 'in Christ' and
policies adopted in the Church. However, he does not argue for
these in two of the three areas mentioned, and this makes the verse's
meaning uncertain. Attempted solutions centre on the probability
that Paul in this verse is quoting a baptismal liturgy; on the probable
echo of Genesis 1.27 in the switch to 'male *and* female'; and on the
significance of his dropping the phrase at 1 Corinthians 12.13 and
(if by Paul) Colossians 3.10. It is possible that the (hypothetical)
original formula considers distinctions that carried weight in the
old order abolished in the new. Even Paul can say that 'in Christ
there is new creation' (or 'a new creature': 2 Corinthians 5.17),
and some of the Corinthians' behaviour would be explicable as
unisex implications drawn from such a belief. Jesus also may have
been understood to deny gender difference in the new age (Mark
12.25), which the Corinthians apparently thought they had already
entered.

It is instructive that Paul can (probably) quote a tradition that
he is not entirely happy with, and also in effect criticise it. Modern
interpreters do the same. But there is no need to follow this
discussion through to any conclusion, because the point is that this
will still be doubtful, and that even if it were strong enough in
principle to bear theological weight, opposite conclusions could be
drawn from it, some arguing that Paul had reservations about the
liturgical tradition, others that he quoted it anyway. Neither side
can draw clear guidance for today, but in the course of discussing
the passage from every possible angle, Christians looking for the

meaning of the gospel in their present local situation may grow in, and come to, the agreement they seek.

At least they can be freed from misusing Scripture in such a way that awkward texts block Christian growth in insight, as when fundamentalists deduce from 1 Corinthians 14.34 that women should not preach (or read the lesson?) in church. 1 Timothy 2.12 is a more serious problem, because less unclear. It is no help to say it is not by Paul, or that 1 Corinthians 14.34 is possibly an interpolation, because they remain part of Scripture. The reason for theological criticism of 1 Timothy 2.11–15 is that theologically speaking (i.e. from the perspective of contemporary Christian faith), it is nonsense, dangerous nonsense, and nonsense on stilts.

Modern theologians convinced of the equality of the sexes must give reasons for discounting those texts[10] which support the subordination of women, reasons based on their understanding of the gospel, which in principle includes their whole understanding of reality. We may conclude with another problem text.

1 Corinthians 11.2–16 is so riddled with exegetical ambiguities that it would in any case be difficult to draw from it firm conclusions about hats or hairstyles, should one wish to do so. But sexual differentiation is insisted upon in an appeal to nature, reinforced by an appeal to scriptural tradition. If anything is warranted by this passage it is sexual differentiation, and as it contradicts the hypothetical pre-canonical meaning of Galatians 3.28, it could reasonably be appealed to against this, if any such neutralisation were necessary. Unfortunately, in the course of casting around in Scripture and experience for arguments in support of what he knows is right as well as expedient, Paul introduced the note of subordination that is frankly incredible to many Christians today. That is present in verses 3 and 7, whatever is meant about the angels in verse 10. Even when the supporting argument of verse 8 ('for a man is not out of a woman but a woman out of a man') is discounted as not helping the case, the offending statements stand, though only as a supporting argument, unable to claim the weight to be accorded to the passage's concern with sexual differentiation. They stem from Paul's culturally conditioned mental furniture and can be set aside without disagreeing with his understanding of the gospel. Unlike Galatians 3.28 they do not belong intrinsically to

an argument about the nature of Christianity. A further cause of relief is verse 11, where the note of reciprocity qualifies the subordination with an insistence on partnership, as at Colossians 3.19. Another is verse 16, where Paul in effect admits that his arguments lack cogency, and falls back on to an appeal to his apostolic authority and general Christian custom. So the note of women's subordination is present, but it cannot be allowed to outweigh our understanding of the gospel, which in the experience of many Christians today demands a new respect for the equality of the sexes.

These brief remarks, bypassing a number of exegetical problems, are intended to suggest that awkward passages can be challenged by critical theological interpretation (whether feminist or any other kind) without denying what they are saying. Their force can be relativised and minimised by setting them (so far as this is possible) in their original context. But the nub of our argument has been to resist a biblicist approach to Scripture while insisting on the centrality of Scripture for hearing the gospel. The gospel is the criterion by which Scripture is assessed, and if necessary we may with Luther 'urge Christ against Scripture'. The biblical theologian who was prepared to do that attended as closely to Scripture as anyone. But he was a theological interpreter, and that means a critical interpreter, one who can tell the difference between the law (or tradition) and the gospel, namely Christ. If a feminist can do that 'she can thank God and know that she is a theologian'.[11]

NOTES

1.   The best discussion of this whole area is D. Kelsey, *The Uses of Scripture in Recent Theology* (Fortress and SCM, 1975).
2.   *In Memory of Her* (SCM Press, London, 1983).
3.   *Summa Theologiae*, 1.1.10, citing Augustine, *Contra Vincent, Donatist.* 48.
4.   See K. Keay (ed.), *Men and Women and God* (Marshall, Morgan and Scott, Basingstoke, 1987).
5.   E.g. E.S. Fiorenza, Rosemary Reuther, Phyllis Bird, Phyllis Trible, Bernadette Brooten, A.Y. Collins, C. Osiek. See A.Y. Collins (ed.)

Feminist Perspectives on Biblical Scholarship (Scholars Press, Chico, 1985) which includes Jewish contributions.

6. E.g. Andrew Kirk, 'Theology from a Feminist Perspective' in K. Keay, op. cit.

7. C. Geertz's essay on 'Religion as a Cultural System' (1963), reprinted in *The Interpretation of Cultures* (Basic Books, New York, 1973), is influential in recent theology.

8. Cf. C.K. Barrett, *Essays on Paul* (SPCK, 1982) pp. 154–70.

9. See D.R. MacDonald, *There is no Male and Female* (Fortress, Philadelphia, 1987) for a full discussion of the alternatives.

10. See also Eph. 5.22–4 and the discussion in J.P. Sampley, *'And the Two Shall Become One Flesh': A Study of Traditions in Eph. 5.21–33* (Cambridge, 1971). 1 Pet. 3.1 is less of a problem because not theologically underwritten.

11. *Weimar Ausgabe* Vol 40, 1; 207, 17f., changing the gender. See G. Ebeling, *Luther* (Fontana, 1972), p. 111. Chapters 6 and 7 are as important for the argument of this essay as is the practice of my other hermeneutics teacher, Ernst Käsemann, whose position on this is usefully explained by B. Ehler, *Die Herrschaft des Gekreuzigten* (De Gruyter, Berlin, 1986), pp. 7–155.

3

Bound by Blood:
Circumcision and Menstrual Taboo
in Post-Exilic Judaism

Léonie J. Archer

The concern of this paper is to explore the possible link between the rites of (male) circumcision[1] and menstrual taboo in the Judaism of the late biblical period. I have for some time been concerned with circumcision – with tracing the evolution of the rite within Judaism and drawing attention to the implications which the lack of a similar or substitute rite had for women in terms of religious and social involvement and activity.[2] Only recently, however, did I begin to perceive a connection between it and the biblical legislation about menstruation and childbirth, and that arose from a rather tardy recognition that (a) central to both is a flow of blood, and (b) covenantal circumcision and the regulations concerning menstruation and childbirth both appeared at the same time and for the first time in the Babylonian exile and beyond (sixth century BC) – that is, according to the still quite widely accepted dating, within the source critical school, of the Priestly document which contains these regulations. (In fact we do not have to rely on the conclusions of this traditional chronological stranding; my argument, as we shall see, independently points to the exile as the time when these rituals would have first emerged.)[3] This simultaneous appearance seemed too much of a coincidence, and prompted me to look a little more closely at it. What emerged from my closer examination is that there is a link, that the two ritual forms are in fact opposite sides of the same coin, and that they derived (at least in their final form) from the trauma of the exile to Babylon and the consequent restructuring of the Jewish community. In the context of the centuries surrounding the exile they served sound, pragmatic patriarchal ends, and in the context of present day Judaism they remain central rituals, with profound resonances for women and their involvement or non-involvement in public religion.[4] In *post hoc* analytical terms, the two rituals may be seen to pivot on perceived gender differentials in blood – i.e. upon an assumed distinction between male blood and female blood – and upon some kind of constructed nature–culture dichotomy – i.e. circumcision being deemed the work of culture and menstruation and childbirth the functioning of nature (in the culturally constructed sense of the word).

My concern, however, is not only to show the, as it were, abstract or theoretically constructed connection between the two groups of legislation, but in more concrete terms, to demonstrate how they both stemmed from and then served to reinforce a changed and inferior position for women in respect to their social and religious involvement and status. In other words, these laws were one aspect of what I perceive to be a negative development in women's lives from the biblical to the post-biblical periods. As indicated already, I believe the exile to have been a turning point or catalyst for both developments, so before turning to the analysis of the two types of ritual practice (for both circumcision and the prescriptions regarding both menstruation and childbirth fall into this category of human activity) it will be necessary, I think, first to sketch in a general picture of the changes which occurred in the religious and social ordering of the Jewish community in the centuries surrounding the exile. This I shall do specifically from the woman's point of view. Thus we shall have both the necessary background in respect to the changing position of women, and the required context for our discussion of these particular rites, for it must be remembered that ritual and ritualistic ideas can only make sense when taken in reference to a total structure of thought and system of social and historical reality (most of which we shall, of course, only be able to touch upon here). They do not spring from a vacuum or according to some arbitrary whim of the people and legislators, but have their origins in the human need to control and order existence. The way in which ritual develops – or, rather, is developed – and the characteristics which it assumes reflect the ordering and preoccupations peculiar to a society. Thus it is essential that we keep in mind that notions which may now seem 'normal' and 'natural' are in fact, as with most things, social and cultural constructs determined by a complex of reasons and situations.

Also by way of introduction and again to be borne in mind in the course of this paper is that nature–culture opposition which I referred to at the start. This framework of analysis is, I am sure, all too familiar – and I am equally sure unacceptable to many. I, however, believe that this universalistic model has much to offer in terms of helping our understanding, and in the context of the present paper may well be of assistance.[5] To remind ourselves of the basic tenets, as it were, of this projected dichotomy: essentially it rests on the assumption that every society recognises a distinction between culture and nature, with ritual being the outer manifestation or expression of this recognition and representing culture's need to regulate and control the passive functioning of its opposite, nature – 'nature', of course, itself being a construct of 'culture'. Regarding the social differentiation between the sexes, this conceptual schematisation can result (and I stress this is just one possibility) in women being perceived as closer to nature in consequence of the biological facts of childbirth and menstruation (or rather, a particular cultural interpretation thereof), whilst men, who are deemed to lack such a cycle of visible creativity (and who have other aspects of their own equally natural physiology denied), are placed within the realm of culture, manipulating their own social and political existence, and transcending the passive forces of nature. Culture, and therefore male activity within this scheme of thought, are consequently seen as superior to nature and female passivity. It should be said that this particular elaboration of the nature–culture split is, of course, also itself a complex social construct and one which serves patriarchal needs in various ways. The split could have gone in a different direction with different characterisations and emphases within the overall framework. To use the nature–culture dichotomy for a greater understanding of a particular situation is not therefore to promote principles of immutable (socio-) biological determinism.[6] Such, then, in extremely broad terms, is the essence of the nature–culture opposition, an opposition which, as I hope to show, provides one clue as to the perceived gender differentials in blood within Judaism which I mentioned at the outset, and which may be of help in establishing an (oppositional) link between circumcision and menstrual taboo.

Turning now to the historical outline of religious and social development. From the early chronological strands of the Old Testament, it is apparent that women in the pre-exilic period of Hebrew history enjoyed a certain active involvement in the nation's religious affairs.[7] In the biblical narratives they appear as singers, dancers, prophetesses, sacred prostitutes, and in other cultic capacities. Significantly, however, the period to which these texts refer was one in which that rigid monotheism so characteristic of later Judaism had not yet developed. Then, polytheistic belief and worship flourished and shrines to the various deities, which included a number of goddesses, dotted the countryside of Palestine. In the course of time, however, the monotheistic principle began to assert itself, and for a complex of reasons not within the scope of this paper, the god Yahweh was elevated to a position of supremacy over all other deities. With this rise to power of a single male deity and the concomitant lessening in status of the other members of the Israelite pantheon (especially its female members), the role played by women in public religion began to diminish. The first step in that direction was taken when the early Hebrew legislators forbade the practice of sacred prostitution, this ritual being fundamental to the non-Yahwistic cults and also one in which women played a central role. Women were further removed from cultic activity when the Yahwists forced the abolition of all rural shrines in Palestine and centralised worship at the Temple in Jerusalem, a move which was again designed to rid the land of undesirable cults. At this central sanctuary there was no place for female officiants as the Temple's affairs were regarded as the sole responsibility of an organised, hereditary male priesthood dedicated to the service of Yahweh. But, despite all efforts, worship of the old gods and goddesses continued throughout the land of Israel and even on occasion at the Temple of Jerusalem itself – as evidenced by the books of Kings and Chronicles, which refer to events of the seventh and sixth centuries.

Ironically, Yahweh's final victory came with the destruction of his Temple at the hands of the Babylonians in 587 BC. For generations prior to this calamity the custodians and promoters of Yahweh – that is, the now canonised Prophets of Israel – had been warning the people that if they did not abandon their syncretistic ways, the wrath of the one true God would descend upon them. For the people as a whole, therefore, the destruction of the Temple and the exile to Babylon came to be viewed as dramatic realisation of these doom prophecies, and proof of the absolute power of the jealous god Yahweh, and – harnessing these concepts to their own pragmatic ends – the exiles set about ridding themselves of all impurity in an effort to regain his favour. To this end all records of the past were zealously preserved and older, more primitive legal traditions extensively reworked and edited in the light of developing concepts and attitudes – most of which would seem to have been the direct result of the community's change in circumstances and new needs for order and social cohesion.[8] Of particular significance and far-reaching consequence to the lives of women was the exilic legislators' obsession with ritual cleanness[9] – and in order to understand the full import of this statement, I shall momentarily have to digress from our historical outline and spend a little time analysing the reasons for the legislators' obsession and its impact.

Remembering that we are here dealing with a community first in exile and then returned to an impoverished and divided land (i.e. Palestine towards the end of the sixth and in the course of the fifth centuries BC),[10] it is significant that the principal concern of the Priestly Code was with the laws of *kashrut*, pollutions from secretions from various bodily orifices, and legislation about the cult and priesthood.[11] This concern for purity and order – for that is what the legislation is about – both reflected society's concern for its own racial integrity and social cohesion, and in turn served to promote them. As Mary Douglas writes:

> The idea of society is a powerful image . . . This image has form; it has external boundaries, margins, structure . . . For symbols of society any human experience of structure, margins, or boundaries is ready to hand.[12]

And again:

> . . . ideas about separating, purifying, demarcating and punishing transgressions have as their main function to impose system on an inherently untidy experience. It is only by exaggerating the difference between within and without, above and below, male and female, with and against, that a semblance of order is created.[13]

So, for example, the laws of *kashrut*, whilst serving an obvious pragmatic purpose of separating and distinguishing the Jews from their neighbours, and guarding against assimilation, also served to affirm the selected symbolic system, the abomination and avoidance of crawling things being the negative side of the pattern of things approved and a function of the ordering of society.[14] Similarly, the concern for the pollution of and from bodily secretions on a practical level worked to promote the integrity and productivity (in human terms) of the family unit – a matter of prime importance for a group concerned for its very existence and reproduction – whilst on a symbolic level, the exiles' concentration upon the unity, purity and integrity of the physical body well reflected their larger concern for the threatened boundaries of the body politic. The overt rationale behind the new prescriptions was the desire to create a people which was truly holy to God.[15]

Whilst the laws of ritual purity were directed at both men and women,[16] women – in order to promote practical, patriarchal socio-economic concerns – were particularly affected.[17] Central to the legislators' notions of purity was an all-pervasive blood taboo (which embraced foodstuffs; sacrificial victims; humans, etc., and very definitely separated out the male from the female). The fact that, unlike men, women's periods of bodily emission followed a regular and extended (i.e. several days at a time) cycle meant that they were declared unclean for a large part of their lives (for details see below). Great attention was paid to the pollution which resulted from contact with them during these periods, with vital purification rituals being prescribed to avert the danger to both individuals and community (in particular, the *male religious community* – see below). For, to take just one aspect of this notion of danger, just as crawling things could be seen as the negative side of things approved, so the flow of female blood, again in symbolic terms, could be seen as the negative side of the ideal concept of society as whole and self-contained.[18] In other words, whilst necessary to the system on both practical and symbolic levels, and a strengthening factor to the positive definition, it remained also an offence to the ideal, marginal to the correct order, and therefore dangerous. (It was also of course a source of female power.[19]) In addition to the prescriptions of purification ritual, further precautions were taken by severely restricting the movement of women during their times of uncleanness, particularly with regard to their access to or participation in cultic affairs – matters to which I shall return shortly.

Before turning to my next point in the historical outline, I would also like quickly to note the way in which this new notion of female impurity rapidly made inroads into the popular imagination, with the result that women came to be seen as a constant stumbling block to man's improvement, a blight on the possibility of his attaining the now required (i.e. post-exilic) standard of personal purity. So, for example, in the fourth century BC, Job could write:

> Man that is born of woman is of few days and full of trouble . . .
> Who can bring a clean thing out of an unclean?
> What is man that he should be clean?
> And he that is born of woman that he should be righteous?

> (Job 14.1,3;15.4)

It was an easy step from this type of attitude to regard women as the source of all evil in the world, and that indeed is what happened in the exile and beyond when there emerged the concept of the Evil Woman, of wickedness personified in female form. Such developments, however, are the concern of another paper.[20]

Returning to our historical outline and intimately connected with this new notion of female impurity, was the development of an increased rigidity in attitude towards and definition of function within the family group – something which had gradually been happening before the sixth century but which was accelerated and refined by the experience of the exile.[21] Together with moves towards greater urbanisation, more complex economic systems, shifts in societal and familial structure (in particular the movement away from the earlier extended family unit to the nucleated one), there developed the situation whereby the woman's role was placed firmly and almost exclusively in the private sphere of activity as wife, mother and homemaker (a removal encouraged by the purity laws), whilst that of the man was located in the public sphere as worker and family supporter, and active participant in social, political and religious affairs. This sharp differentiation, and the various impulses and societal shifts which encouraged it, (which unfortunately we do not have space to go into here) was quite different to the situation which pertained in earlier Hebrew history. In religious terms, these two exilic and post-exilic developments – i.e. the concentration upon ritual purity and the sharp differentiation in male–female social function – were to have far-reaching consequences for women. Henceforth they were denied access to active participation in the public cult and (by implication of the biblical text which concentrated upon male activity) deemed exempt from the obligation to fulfil many of the commandments – a loaded exemption given the fact that Judaism by this time was already very much a religion of performance, moving towards being a religion dominated by a plethora of commandments governing virtually every aspect of daily existence.[22] This implication was later firmed up by the Sages of the Second Commonwealth to become a fully fledged rabbinic declaration of exemption embracing nearly all of the positive commandments whose fulfilment depended upon a specific time of the day or of the year – an exemption which rapidly came to be viewed in terms of actual exclusion. So, for example, women were under no obligation to circumcise their sons (a point of some significance in the context of the present paper, and one to which I shall return later), or take them to the Temple for the ritual redemption of the first-born;[23] they were exempt from making the thrice yearly pilgrimage to Jerusalem at the feasts of Passover, Pentecost and Tabernacles; from living in the ceremonial booths at *Sukkoth*; shaking the *lulab*; sounding the *shofar*; and even, at a later stage, of pronouncing the daily affirmation of faith, the *Shema*. Women's exemption from these time-geared precepts was the result both of their extensive periods of ritual impurity and of their designated role as closeted homemakers – though of course in making such a statement, we immediately involve ourselves in a great degree of circularity. Unclean, and in a state of domestic seclusion, they thus became increasingly less involved in matters of public religion, and the situation quickly developed wherein their non-participation was viewed in term of actual exclusion rather than mere exemption.[24] Now, therefore, and unlike the earlier period, only men were the full participants in and officiants of the nation's religious life. In other words, they comprised the religious community; they were the sons of the new covenant as developed in the exile and beyond.

The mark of this new covenant was (and still is) circumcision. Circumcision as a rite had been performed in Israel for many centuries, but it was only with the exile that it assumed the character of a covenantal sign between God and his chosen people. Prior to that it had been viewed in terms of an individual's placatory act of redemption to the deity (or deities) and later as a rite of initiation into the tribe, so marking the male's passage firstly to ordinary, profane existence and secondly to full, public and potentially active membership of society.[25] Already at this stage of the rite's evolution, the absence of a similar rite or substitute ceremony for the girl was a loaded omission. But it was the final stage in the history of circumcision which was to have the most far-reaching implications for the woman and her role in the society and religion of her people. In the exile it was decreed that circumcision was to be *the* official rite of initiation into Judaism and all that that now meant. It is in Genesis 17.10ff – verses which are usually taken as belonging to the Priestly strand of the Bible – that we first find mention of the covenantal aspect of circumcision:

And God said unto Abraham . . . This is My Covenant, which ye shall keep between Me and you and thy seed after thee: every male among you shall be circumcised. And ye shall be circumcised in the flesh of your foreskin; and it shall be a token of a covenant betwixt Me and you. And he that is eight days old[26] shall be circumcised among you, every male throughout your generations, he that is born in thy house, or bought with the money of any foreigner, that is not of thy seed . . . And the uncircumcised male who is not circumcised in the flesh of his foreskin, that soul shall be cut off from his people; he hath broken my covenant.

Henceforth, and unlike the earlier period, this was to be the dominant aspect of the rite. Now it was not simply the male, but the circumcised male who was to be the full participant in his nation's covenantal law and cultic activities. So, for example, with regard to observance of the Passover, the pre-exilic ruling was for 'thee and thy son', with no further qualification, to keep the feast, whereas in the exilic and post-exilic legislation the ordinance was modified to count only those who had been circumcised.[27] Similarly, only circumcised men were under an obligation to fulfil the whole law[28] – and we should recall that the essence of Judaism was now legalism and observance of the commandments. In other words, they formed the public religious community, and so the words covenant and circumcision are often used interchangeably in the post-exilic writings.[29]

Another aspect of this later circumcision of particular pertinence to the present discussion is that removal of the foreskin did not on its own render the rite effective. Tremendous importance was attached to the actual blood of the circumcision, and unless several drops of blood were seen to issue from the wound, the operation was deemed invalid and valueless. Later it was even specified that should there be for any reason no foreskin to sever, blood must still be made to flow for the rite to be effective and for the individual to enter the covenant.[30] Whilst blood would appear to have been associated with circumcision from the earliest times (witness the account of Zipporah),[31] this character of the rite, as I hope shortly to show, assumed new dimensions and significances with the experience of the exile and the developments which I have just outlined.

As a clue to that significance we might recall firstly the way in which the laws regarding menstruation and childbirth and this new circumcision appeared at the same time in the history of the Jewish people, and secondly what I said earlier about the need of culture to control or impose itself upon what it deems to be nature. Before entering upon that comparative analysis, however, I would first like to indicate the general significance which blood – of certain types – had within Hebrew thought and society; and then, within that context, point to the particular significance of its shedding in the rite of circumcision.

Firstly, blood was perceived to be the life-giving force of the universe – an obvious conclusion on empirical grounds, but one which was then elevated from the pragmatic to the sacred in Hebrew thought by the belief that in humans it was also the seat of the soul.[32] Hence prohibitions on and descriptions of killing in the Bible were couched specifically in terms of the shedding of another's blood.[33] Secondly, the blood of animals was also considered sacred, or at least as belonging particularly to the deity (hence the prohibition on humans eating it),[34] and so animal sacrifice and the dashing of their blood played an all-pervasive role in the Jewish cult, being regarded as a means of atoning for sins, purging ritual impurity, and connecting with the God-head.[35] Differences were made regarding the value of male sacrifices as opposed to female ones, the latter only being offered on less important or non-community based occasions.[36] We might also note the way in which this cultic shedding of blood was controlled by men, and the fact that in the exilic ordinances regarding sacrificial procedure – contained in the Priestly strands of Exodus – the consecration of Aaron and his sons to the priesthood was marked by the daubing of blood upon their right ears, thumbs and feet.[37] Thirdly, and following these first two points, it was also believed that to shed one's own blood ritually and voluntarily – and I stress the word 'voluntarily' – was to recommend oneself to and establish a link with the Creator of the Universe – and this is precisely what happened with circumcision.[38] In other words, by the culture-controlled shedding of blood at circumcision, the individual entered the covenant and joined with his fellow 'circumcisees', who together formed a community or brotherhood of blood, bound to each other and God by special duties and mutual obligations. Most importantly, this brotherhood was seen as extending laterally across a generation, vertically to fathers, grandfathers, sons and grandsons, and ultimately to God – a point to which I shall return.[39] The new significance of the covenantal blood of circumcision was clearly demonstrated by the later midrashic paraphrase of 'life is in the blood' to 'life is in the blood of circumcision'.[40]

At precisely the same time as circumcision and the blood of circumcision were receiving this new casting and additional dimension, legislation about female blood – i.e. the blood of menstruation and childbirth – appeared for the first time on the scene. But the attention paid to it was of a completely different nature to that accorded male blood. As we have seen, *it* was declared unclean and ritually polluting, and was equated metaphorically with the defilement imparted by carrying an idol.[41] Unlike the cultic *inclusion* of men through the blood of circumcision, the blood of the female cycle resulted in cultic *exclusion* for women. So, according to the laws of Leviticus, women were forbidden to enter the Temple or touch any hallowed thing during their times of menstrual uncleanness,[42] whilst with regard to childbirth they were similarly removed from cultic activity, this time for forty days following delivery of a boy and significantly eighty days after that of a girl.[43] And here I would like to quote the Levitical ruling on childbirth for it highlights what I hope is now becoming clear, i.e. the perceived gender differentials in blood and the connection between male circumcision and the female blood cycle:

If a woman be delivered and bear a man-child, then she shall be unclean seven days; as in the days of the impurity of her sickness shall she be unclean.

And in the eighth day the flesh of his foreskin shall be circumcised.

And she shall continue in the blood of purification three and thirty days; she shall touch no hallowed thing, nor come into the sanctuary, until the days of her purification be fulfilled.

But if she bear a maid-child, then she shall be unclean two weeks, as in her impurity; and she shall continue in the blood of purification threescore and six days.

And when the days of her purification are fulfilled, for a son or for a daughter, she shall bring a lamb of the first year for a burnt offering, and a young pigeon or a turtle dove, for a sin offering, unto the door of the tent of meeting, unto the priest.

After Eve

> And he shall offer it before the Lord, and make atonement for her; and she shall be cleansed from the fountain of her blood . . . the priest shall make atonement for her, and she shall become clean (Lev. 12.2ff.).

The main points to note from this passage are firstly the way in which the blood of delivery is unclean; secondly the way in which in the case of a boy's birth, circumcision intrudes in the text and interrupts both the period of the mother's pollution and the account of that pollution; and thirdly, the way in which the woman is finally cleansed of her impurity through the blood of sacrifice as administered by a circumcised male.

It is apparent, therefore, that differentiation was made between male and female blood, and that circumcision, in its new casting, had some role to play in that context. To deal with the blood differential first: according to the later thinking of the tannaim (rabbis of the first centuries AD), the reason for the Levitical laws of menstruation and childbirth was as punishment for the sin of Eve who brought about the death of Adam. In other words, '. . . because she shed his blood, she was punished through her blood'.[44] As the quotation shows, the two types of blood were perceived as two sides of the same coin: on the one side positive male blood and on the other negative female blood. However, whilst the image of the 'head and tail' coin is pertinent to our understanding of the rituals, the rabbis' words provide us with little more than an appreciation of how Jewish society (or a part thereof) at the time perceived and explained the religious state of affairs. In other words, they merely represent a constructed rationale of an existing custom.[45] To reach a fuller understanding of the blood differential – its origin, purpose and effect – it is necessary to dig a little deeper and attempt to trace the underlying reasons by means of a sociological/anthropological analysis – and this is what I have been attempting to do in the course of this paper. I would now like to reiterate and elaborate the several points which I have raised so far, and then finally bring my argument round to demonstrating the link which exists between circumcision and menstrual/childbirth taboos.

The first point is that it is generally recognised that ritual tends to increase, intensify and shift in focus at times of social crisis. In particular – and on this see the work of Mary Douglas – when the body politic is threatened, it is common to see increased attention paid to the purity, integrity and unity of the physical body.[46] This, as we have seen, is precisely what happened with the exile and in the Levitical legislation regarding ritual pollution.

Secondly, ritual, in addition to mirroring the anxieties of society, also expresses the ordering of society in all its aspects and complexity, and to use the words of Ortner, may be viewed as marking the universal human endeavour to transcend and control the world of nature (amongst other things). Indeed, to continue with Ortner's words, 'the distinctiveness of culture rests precisely on the fact that it can under most circumstances transcend natural conditions and turn them to its purpose. Thus culture at some level of awareness asserts itself to be not only distinct from but superior to nature, and that sense of distinctiveness and superiority rests precisely on the ability to transform – to "socialise" and "culturalise" – nature',[47] i.e. to be active and in control.

Within this scheme of thought, anything which cannot be controlled is labelled dangerous and marginal, particularly when society is working to preserve its unity and to develop more sophisticated systems of self-definition, as was the case for the Jewish community in Palestine following the exile. The blood of childbirth and menstruation, which follows a passive and unstoppable cycle, can be construed (by the powers that be) to fall within this category, and so it is required that cultural regulation step in with restrictive legislation. That cultural regulation, as we have seen, is controlled by men, for (and this brings me to the third point) within this scheme of thought, woman herself is placed more fully within the realm of nature than man in consequence of the fact that more of her time and her body are seen to be taken up with the natural processes surrounding reproduction of the species.[48] Man, on the other hand, who within this particular characterisation of the nature–culture dichotomy is deemed to lack such natural and visible creative functions, is obliged, or at least has the opportunity (to use the words of Ortner) to assert his creativity externally through the medium of technology, ritual and symbol.[49] As active manipulator of his existence, he falls within the realm of culture, and so, just as culture is deemed superior to nature, so man and his activities are considered superior to woman and her world.[50]

And this brings me to my fourth point, and that is the notion of domestic–public opposition. Following the exile, it should be recalled that women, for a complex of pragmatic reasons, were confined almost exclusively to the domestic realm. This relegation – for as such it was construed[51] – to the domestic realm, whilst on the one hand promoting a higher status than before for women in terms of motherhood (a status generated for society's structural purposes and needs[52]), also resulted in an overall decrease in women's status generally for, to use the well known Levi-Straussian model, the domestic unit – i.e. the 'biological' family concerned with reproducing and socialising new members of society[53] – was seen as separate from the public entity, i.e. the superimposed network of alliances and relationships which comprised society proper, as it were. And this separation – or indeed opposition – according to Levi-Strauss, had the significance of the opposition between nature and culture.[54] Women's world could therefore be seen as inferior to the higher cultural activities of men in the public domain[55] – a fact recognised by the first-century AD Jewish philosopher Philo who in his writings made much play of this gender-differentiated opposition between the public and private domains.[56] The same writer also pointed to a prime offshoot of this particular nature–culture dichotomy when he wrote, in the context of explaining why the male sacrificial victim is preferable to the female, that:

> virtue is male since it causes movement and affects conditions and suggests noble conceptions of noble deeds and words . . . the male is more complete, more dominant than the female, closer akin to causal activity, for the female is incomplete and in subjection and belongs to the category of the passive rather than the active (*Abraham* 102; *Spec. Leg.* 1.200).

And this brings me finally to the link between circumcision and menstrual taboo.

Whilst women's role as mothers was of paramount importance to society – particularly after the exile when maternity, for various pragmatic reasons, became the means of transmitting and establishing in biological terms, as it were, religious and ethnic identity[57] – it would seem logical, given our culture–nature opposition and the fact that culture seeks to control and impose upon whatever has been construed as natural, that something had to be done in cultural terms about the natural function of childbirth. And this, I think, is where circumcision comes in. It served as a rite of cultural rebirth by which the male individual was accorded entry into the society and religion of his people. In other words, whilst women, as it were, merely conducted the animal-like repetitive tasks of carrying on the reproduction of the human race, men, by one supreme symbolic act, imposed themselves upon nature and enacted a cultural rebirth. The blood of circumcision served as a symbolic surrogate for the blood of childbirth, and because it was shed voluntarily and in a controlled manner, it transcended the bounds of nature and the passive blood flow of the mother at delivery and during the preparatory cycle for pregnancy, menstruation.[58] The blood of circumcision, just like the blood of animal sacrifice, could also be viewed as cleansing the boy of his mother's blood and acting as a rite of separation, differentiating him from the female, and allying him with the male community.[59] In a sense, therefore, circumcision actually creates a more powerful gender distinction rather than just deriving from such a distinction – but here again one gets wrapped in inevitable strands of circularity. For all of these reasons, and unlike the earlier biblical period, only men were allowed to perform the operation.[60] At a later time it was even decreed that should there be no male (in particular a father) available to sever the foreskin and make the blood flow, then the child should wait until he had grown up and then perform the operation himself. Under no circumstances was the mother to enact this cultural role.[61] All of this was so very different from the earlier period of Hebrew history when the first recorded occasion of a circumcision had as its central active character the woman Zipporah.

In conclusion, then, natural birth gave rise to an intergenerational line of blood; cultural rebirth created a network or brotherhood of blood which transcended generations and was superior to biological and socio-biological kinship ties. These were the two sides of the same coin which I referred to at the beginning of my paper, the nature–culture opposition and the particular characterisations and choice of emphases here explored being one explanation for the apparent gender differentials in blood within Jewish ritual practice, and one link at least between the rite of circumcision and menstrual taboo in post-exilic Judaism.

BIBLE

Chron.	Chronicles
Deut.	Deuteronomy
Exod.	Exodus
Ezek.	Ezekiel
Gen.	Genesis
Lam.	Lamentations
Lev.	Leviticus

TALMUD

Ab. Zarah	Abodah Zarah
Hull.	Hullin
Kidd.	Kiddushin
Shabb.	Shabbat
Pes.	Pesahim
Yeb.	Yebamoth

MIDRASH

Gen. R.	Genesis Rabbah

PHILO

Spec. Leg.	Specialibus Legibus (Special Laws)
Abrahm	De Abrahmo (on Abraham)

JOSEPHUS

Con. Ap.	Contra Apionem (Against Apion)

NOTES

1. The only form of circumcision practised among the Hebrews/Jews: Strabo is certainly incorrect in his view that both male and female children were circumcised (*Geographica*, XVI, 2:37, 4:9; XVII, 2:5). Even if he were correct it is clear from surveys of other cultures that female circumcision has a very different function to the male rite with which we are here concerned. On this point, see Nawal El Saadawi, *The Hidden Face of Eve. Women in the Arab World* (London, 1980).
2. See Léonie J. Archer, *Her Price is beyond Rubies. The Jewish Woman in Graeco-Roman Palestine* (Sheffield, 1990), Ch. I, sect. b.

3. For a history of source criticism and other methodological approaches to the Old Testament, in particular the Pentateuch, see Douglas A. Knight and Gene M. Tucker (eds), *The Hebrew Bible and Its Modern Interpreters* (Philadelphia and Chico, 1985), especially Ch. 8. For details regarding recent debates over the dating of the Priestly literature (which varies from pre-Deuteronomic to Persian, but with the majority of scholars still looking to the exilic and post-exilic age) and discussion as to whether P is a source or redaction, see ibid. especially pp. 285–6.

4. Regarding circumcision it is significant to note that one of the five objections to the ritual raised by leaders of the nineteenth century Reform Movement in Frankfurt was the fact that there was no initiation for daughters into Judaism.

5. This model was first developed by Sherry Ortner to help account for the universal subordination or secondary status of women in all societies at all times. See her 'Is Female to Male as Nature is to Culture?' in Michelle Zimbalist Rosaldo and Louise Lamphere (eds), *Women, Culture and Society* (Stanford, 1974), pp. 67–87. Opponents of her argument who are disinclined to use any universalistic model and who argue that Ortner simply swapped one set of deterministic principles (biological) for another equally inflexible set (social constructionist) include Janet Sayers, *Biological Politics* (London, 1982) and Carol P. MacCormack, 'Nature, Culture and Gender: A Critique' in Carol MacCormack and Marilyn Strathern (eds) *Nature, Culture and Gender* (Cambridge, 1980), pp. 1–24. The model here presented and then applied is a modified version of Ortner's which attempts to avoid some of the obvious pitfalls of her early argument whilst at the same time acknowledging its debt to her work.

6. See Ortner, op. cit. p. 71, '[biological] facts and differences only take on significance of superior/inferior within the framework of culturally defined value systems'; Kirsten Hastrup, p. 49, 'socially significant distinctions are mapped on to basic biological differences and vice versa' ('The Semantics of Biology: Virginity', in Shirley Ardener (ed.) *Defining Females* (London, 1978), pp. 49–65); and MacCormack, op. cit. p. 18, 'the link between nature and women is not a "given". Gender and its attributes are not pure biology. The meanings attributed to male and female are as arbitrary as are the meanings attributed to nature and culture.'

7. For details of this involvement and the subsequent developments here itemised, with biblical references and bibliography, see Léonie J. Archer, 'The Role of Jewish Women in the Religion, Ritual and Cult of Graeco-Roman Palestine' in Averil Cameron and Amelie Kuhrt (eds), *Images of Women in Antiquity* (London, 1983), pp. 273–87.

8. Or at least if not the direct result they received their final and decisive impulse from the experience of the exile. Religious and social ordering had been slowly changing in the immediately preceding

After Eve

centuries, but the exile both accelerated and fixed these developments and marked a definite turning point. On this see further below and Léonie J. Archer, 'The Virgin and the Harlot in the Writings of Formative Judaism', *History Workshop Journal* issue 24 (Autumn 1987), pp. 1–16.

9. In saying that these laws were in fact exilic, I again follow both the traditional dating within the documentary hypothesis framework and, more importantly, the internal dynamic or logic of the sociological argument here elucidated.

10. Note that only the elite of the nation had been taken into exile by Nebuchadnezzar, leaving behind 'vinedressers, husbandmen, and the poorest sort of the people of the land' (2 Kings 24.14; 25.12). Of these exiles only a portion then returned to the land to start the process of purification and separation. For this see the accounts of Ezra and Nehemiah.

11. See Mary Douglas, *Purity and Danger* (London, 1966), p. 124, for the way in which concern about orifices, fluids, etc., mirrors the anxieties of a 'hard-pressed minority'.

12. Op. cit. p. 114.

13. Ibid. p. 4. Of particular importance to us here, of course, is the need to create distinct male–female categories.

14. For an analysis of the dietary laws along these lines, see Douglas, op. cit., Ch. 3.

15. See the constant admonitions to this effect in Ezra, Nehemiah and throughout the priestly strands of the OT, particularly Leviticus. For the equation by the legislators of ritual cleanness with holiness, see Jacob Neusner, *The Idea of Purity in Ancient Judaism*, with a critique and commentary by Mary Douglas (Leiden, 1983).

16. The rules specific to men concerned excretions from the sexual organs (i.e. venereal disease) and issues of semen (Lev. 15.3–18). The first necessitated counting 'seven days for his cleansing' whilst the second, obviously more common state resulted in impurity only 'until the even', i.e. the first sunset following the emission. The rules which pertained specifically to women will be treated below.

17. Douglas argues (op. cit. p. 101) that women are particularly affected because their bodies serve as biological models or symbols for the purity of society – and so by implication they are the special target of such legislation. The dangers of such an argument are, however, all too obvious in that it implies an inescapable destiny for women. I prefer the focus here taken which emphasises both the socio-economic dynamic and the *cultural* mapping on to the biological, in particular the *patriarchal* cultural mapping.

18. Here again, unlike Douglas et al., I would stress that this is just one possible interpretation of the biological facts. See pp. 40f above.

19. By virtue of the fact that anything that threatens also wields power.

Female danger/power also rested on the fact of women occupying structurally marginal positions (i.e. neither fully inside nor outside the system, not wholly nature nor culture) and on the fact that society placed them in interstructural roles (as wives and daughters) with respect to alliance making and linking disparate power groups. Although officially accorded little or no power, therefore, it may be seen that women's culturally ambiguous position within Hebrew patriarchy resulted in a type of informal sub-structural power dynamic which in turn regenerated the culturally constructed fear of women necessary to patriarchal interests and explicit power concerns.

20. For the rise of this concept/image and its use in creating distinct gender categories and social roles, see Archer, 'The Virgin and the Harlot in the Writings of Formative Judaism', *History Workshop Journal* issue 24 (Autumn 1987), pp. 1–16.

21. For details of this evolution, which can only be touched upon here, and the sharp impulse provided by the exile see Archer, *Her Price is Beyond Rubies*, Ch. 1 Sect. d.

22. For the way in which the law was the hallmark of Judaism – a situation very different to the earlier Hebrew religion – see idem and 'The Role of the Jewish Woman in the Religion, Ritual and Cult of Graeco-Roman Palestine', p. 277.

23. For details of this and the other exemptions, with full rabbinic references and secondary source citation, see 'The Role of the Jewish Woman in the Religion, Ritual and Cult of Graeco-Roman Palestine', pp. 277ff.

24. As much is implied by various writers of the period (see *Her Price is Beyond Rubies*, Ch. 1, Sect. d). Note also the rabbinic view that if a woman did perform a commandment from which she was 'exempt', the action was without value for she was as 'one who is not commanded and fulfills' (*Sot.* 21a).

25. For this early history plus details of the rite's subsequent development, see Archer, *Her Price is Beyond Rubies*, Ch. 1, Sect. b.

26. For the significance of the operation being performed on the eighth day of the child's life rather than at any other time, see idem.

27. Contrast Exod. 12.24 (J) with Exod. 12.43 (P). Cf. Exod. 23.17; 34.23; Deut. 16.17, all of which are pre-exilic.

28. See, for example, the later statement of Gal. 5.3. Note also the way in which God-fearers who attached themselves to the Jewish community but who were not under an obligation to fulfil the whole law were characterised by various ancient writers as 'the uncircumcised' (see Emil Schürer, *The History of the Jewish People in the Age of Jesus Christ* (eds G. Vermers, F. Millar, M. Goodman, Edinburgh, 1987), III.2, pp. 165ff.

29. It should be said that the uncircumcised Jew remained a Jew by birth (see *Hull.* 4b; *Ab. Zarah* 27a, and n. 57 below), but he was denied

access to the higher life, as it were, of his people (i.e. like a woman). The penalty for non-observance of the rite was *karet* (Gen. 17.14) which was interpreted by the rabbis to mean premature death at the hands of heaven.

30.   *Shabb.* 135–7; *Yeb.* 71a; *Gen. R.* 46:12, 'The sages have taught thus: in the case of an infant born without a foreskin it is necessary *to cause a few drops of the blood of the covenant to flow from him on account of the covenant of Abraham.*' All the texts refer to 'the blood of the covenant'. On this and the sacrificial character of the rite, see Geza Vermes, *Scripture and Tradition in Judaism* (Leiden, 1961), pp. 190–91.

31.   Exod. 4.24–6, 'And it came to pass on the way at the lodging place that the Lord met him [Moses] and sought to kill him. Then Zipporah [Moses's wife] took a flint and cut off the foreskin of her son and cast it at his [Moses's/angel's?] feet, and she said ''Surely a bridegroom of blood art thou to me . . . A bridegroom of blood in regard to circumcision.'' ' Later sources (Targum, Septuagint) also emphasise the all-important role which the blood of circumcision had in Moses's redemption. On the complexities of this passage and its treatment by post-biblical writers, see Vermes, op. cit., pp. 180ff. and H. Kosmala, 'The Bloody Husband', *Vetus Testamentum* 12 (1962).

32.   Lev. 17.11, 14 and see n. 35 below.

33.   See *Jewish Encyclopaedia*, vol. III, p. 259.

34.   Lev. 3.17; 7.26; 17.10–14; 19.26; Deut. 12.16,23; 15.23.

35.   So in context of the divine prohibition on human consumption of animal blood we read, 'For the life of the flesh is in the blood; and I have given it to you upon the altar to make atonement for your souls . . .' (Lev. 17.11). For the way in which the blood of sacrifice was daubed, smeared, sprinkled and generally offered as a means of covenanting, consecrating, expiating, purging, etc., see Leviticus *passim* and the Priestly strands of Exodus. See also the way in which the later book of Hebrews saw as the hallmark of Judaism Temple activity and the cultic shedding of blood (9.13ff. NB the theme continued in Christianity in that the basis of the new covenant was also blood – that of the male redeemer Christ, the ultimate sacrifice).

36.   For a useful breakdown of the sacrificial procedure in terms of the victim's sex, see Judah Ben-Siyyon Segal, *The Hebrew Passover from the Earliest Times to AD 70* (London, 1963), pp. 141–2 (though beware the purely pragmatic reasons which he adduces for the hierarchy). More importantly, see the statement made by Philo regarding the cult's preference for the male (*Spec. Leg.* I. 198ff., quoted in part below, p. 52) and note also that regarding sacrifice/redemption of firstlings only the male was counted.

37.   Exod. 29.12ff.

38.   Strictly speaking of course the eight-day-old child could not 'voluntarily' shed his own blood, but the assumption was that if he

were able to determine his own fate, he would so choose. In any case, whether it was the child's will or not, the event still marked the operation of culture over nature, albeit in this instance through the agency of others.

39. So, for example, see Mal. 2.10 ('Have we not all one father? Hath not one God created us? Why do we deal treacherously every man against his brother, profaning the covenant of our fathers?'); Amos 1.9 (the 'brotherly covenant', *berith achim*); Ezekiel 18.4 ('Behold all souls are mine; as the soul of the father is mine, so also the soul of the son is mine').

40. *Midrash Rabbah*, Lev. 17.11. Note also the way in which both midrashic and targumic exegesis saw Israel as having been saved through the blood of passover *and* the blood of circumcision. See Vermes, op. cit., pp. 190–91.

41. So, for example, the statement of R. Akiba in *Shabb*. 9:1. For biblical instances of the uncleanness of the menstruant being used as a noun and metaphor for the height of defilement, see Ezek. 7.19–20; Lam. 1.17; Ezra 9.11; 2 Chron. 29.5 (note the dates of these works).

42. Lev. 15.19–32. Biblical law declared the woman unclean just for the days of bleeding, up until the close of a seven day period (if bleeding continued thereafter she entered a different category of uncleannness); rabbinic law, however, extended the period of uncleanness to count from the day the woman expected her menses through to the close of seven clear days (i.e. days without bleeding), and totalled the whole period of impurity as a minimum of twelve days. The emphasis of the biblical law (our concern here) was with admission to the cult, that of the rabbis with sexual activity between husband and wife. For details of the consequences of impurity, its transmission to others, etc., see *Encyclopaedia Judaica*, vol. 12, cols 1141–7; vol. 13, cols 1405–12.

43. For an analysis of the social significance of this differentiation, see Archer, *Her Price is Beyond Rubies*, Ch. I, Sect. b.

44. *Gen. Rabbah* 17:13.

45. Here it is significant to note that in the main Eve is *not* cited as the culprit for the Fall, rather the attention of the text lies with Adam. The shift in focus to Eve only came about with Christianity and the work of the Church Fathers. On this see Archer, 'The Virgin and the Harlot in the Writings of Formative Judaism', p. 2 and n. 5.

46. Op. cit., especially Chs 7 and 9.

47. Op. cit., pp. 72–3.

48. See Simone de Beauvoir, *The Second Sex*, pp. 24ff. regarding the non-function to the individual of breasts, ovarian secretions, menstrual cycle, etc., and her conclusion (p. 239) that the female '. . . is more enslaved to the species than the male, her animality is more manifest'. Note the way in which I, along with Ortner (pp. 73ff.), would stress

After Eve

that the woman within this scheme of thought is seen as *closer* to nature and not relegated totally to that realm. As Levi-Strauss writes, no matter how devalued woman and her designated role may be, or how denied her ability to transcend and socialise 'even in a man's world she is still a person, and since insofar as she is defined as a sign she must [still] be recognised as a generator of signs' (*Elementary Structures of Kinship*, ed. R. Needham (Boston, 1969), p. 46). The tensions inherent to this conceptual system and the woman's intermediary and interstructural role are obvious.

49. Op. cit., p. 75.
50. Note in this context de Beauvoir's comments regarding the way in which greater prestige is often accorded the male destruction of life (e.g. warfare, hunting, etc.) than the female creation of life (op. cit., pp. 58–9), and Ortner's comments thereto (p. 75). This is a particularly salient point remembering what has here been said regarding cultic sacrifice and its practitioners.
51. See, for example, Josephus, *Con. Ap.* 2.201; Philo, *Spec. Leg.* 3:169f. (quoted n. 56 below).
52. See the marked frequency with which the community was reminded in the exilic and post-exilic writings of the command to 'Honour thy father and thy mother', and Archer, *Her Price is Beyond Rubies*, Ch. 1, Sect. d and Ch. 3, Sect. a for an analysis of both the commandment's social dynamic and the qualified nature in fact of the respect to be accorded the woman. See also n. 55 below.
53. Levi-Strauss's labelling of the domestic unit as 'biological' is of course too simplistic and indeed predisposes his own conclusion. It is also internally contradictory to his own definition which includes the domestic unit's socialising function. To follow his labelling would be to place women (and other members of the family) totally within the realm of nature. Bearing in mind these drawbacks, though, the model remains extremely useful and insightful.
54. Op. cit., p. 479, quoted in Ortner, op. cit., p. 78.
55. On this see Michelle Zimbalist Rosaldo, 'Woman, Culture, and society: A Theoretical Overview,' in Rosaldo and Lamphere, op. cit. pp. 17–42; Nancy Chodorow, 'Family Structure and Feminine Personality', in ibid., pp. 43–66; Ortner, op. cit. The focus on women's role/status as mother also encouraged this view, for the tendency was to regard the tasks of motherhood as purely natural without recognising that the bulk of the work involved socialising new members of the community.
56. See, for example, Philo *Spec. Leg.* 3:169f., 'Market places and council halls and law courts and gatherings and meetings where a large number of people are assembled, and open air life with full scope for discussion and action – all these are suitable for men both in war and peace. The women are best suited to the indoor life

which never strays from the house . . . Organised communities are of two sorts, the greater which we call cities and the smaller which we call households. Both of these have their governors; the government of the greater is assigned to men under the name of statesmanship, that of the lesser, known as household management, to women . . .'

57.   Regarding the question of Jewish identity, we should note that at least by Talmudic times the (ethnic) status of the child was determined by that of his or her mother and not by the father. So *Kidd.* 68b, 'Thy son by an Israelite woman is called thy son, thy son by a Gentile woman is not called thy son.' According to *Encyclopaedia Judaica*, Vol. 10, cols 54–55, such halachic definition of Jewish identity had been reached by Hasmonaean times. Although more research needs to be done regarding exactly when this understanding of ethnic transmission was introduced, it is certainly possible that it evolved around the time of the exile and the community's return to Palestine.

58.   Although often coming from a completely different analytical perspective to the one here taken, it is interesting and revealing to note the way in which the ritual is popularly described in the secondary sources. For example, E.O. James in *Myth and Ritual* (ed. S.H. Hooke, London, 1933, p. 150) writes, 'In most communities where the corporate attitude of mind still predominates it is necessary for the individual at some period of his [sic] life . . . to undergo a solemn initiation into the tribal society, as distinct from that of the clan or family group in which he has been born. Until this has been done the youth is excluded from the ceremonial (i.e. the social) life of the tribe. Hence the rite consists virtually in a new birth . . . as a complete and active member of society.'

59.   See again Lev. 12.2ff. and my analysis thereof, p. 50 above. See also J.B. Segal, 'Popular Religion in ancient Israel', *Journal of Jewish Studies* 27/1 (Autumn 1976), pp. 5–6, who descriptively rather than analytically writes: 'A male infant was circumcised on the eighth day after birth because he was affected by his mother's uncleanness during the first seven days after the delivery; the eighth day was the first on which he could be approached by the male who carried out the ceremony.'

60.   *Kidd.* 1:7, 29ab; *Pes.* 3:7.

61.   *Kidd.* 1:7, 29ab.

4

Paul and Sexual Identity: 1 Corinthians 11.2–16

Timothy Radcliffe OP

Theologians trying to make sense of St Paul's views on women have been compared to the example that Freud gives of a man defending himself against the accusation of having made a hole in a saucepan that he had borrowed.[1] He argued that he had returned the saucepan intact, and that, anyway, it had had a hole in it when he borrowed it, and indeed he had never borrowed it at all. Similarly theologians will argue that Paul has an admirable theology of women, free of sexism, and anyway he is far less anti-feminist than his contemporaries, and indeed he never wrote the offending texts. I shall look at the most embarrassing Pauline text on women, 1 Corinthians 11.2–16, the passage apparently about the importance of women wearing veils in church, and argue that not only did Paul write it, but that he is tackling a topic of central importance to theology, the relationship between nature and grace. Most of 1 Corinthians is a meditation upon what it means for us to be bodily. In chapter six he looks at the relationship between our bodiliness and sexuality. He explores a theology of our bodiliness that grounds his assertion that it is wrong to sleep with prostitutes.[2] The rest of chapter eleven is devoted to the sharing of the body of Christ; in chapter twelve he will consider what it means for the church to be the Body of Christ, and finally he will look at the importance of belief in the resurrection of the body. The reason why so much of 1 Corinthians focuses on sex and food is that eating and drinking together and sleeping with each other are fundamental expressions of our bodiliness. These two concerns coincide in his discussion of the Eucharist, a meal which is the gift of a body. That is why that passage on the Eucharist is the centre of the letter. In this passage, 11.2–16, Paul is focusing upon one particular aspect of our bodiliness, our sexual identity. What is the relationship between my life as a male, the identity given to me by my nature, and my identity through grace as a member of Christ's Body?

Paul never discusses theological questions out of a purely academic interest. If he explores the relationship between nature and grace with reference to sexual identity, then this must have been a live issue in Corinth. It is very possible that some of the Corinthians had read his letter to the Galatians with enthusiasm: 'There is neither Jew nor Greek, there is neither slave nor free, there is neither male nor female; for you are all one in Christ' (3.28). This could have been taken as a declaration that one should celebrate the gospel by ignoring gender differences. In grace this natural difference is transcended. And we have evidence that many people at Corinth would have been sympathetic to such an interpretation of the gospel. At this time the status of women in Graeco-Roman society was, generally, improving, but they lacked a proper religious expression of their position. Civic religion was dominated by men. This partly accounts for the growing popularity of the mystery religions, for example the cults of Dionysus, Isis and Cybele. For those who were on the margins of civil life, especially women and slaves, these cults offered religious recognition. An interesting article by Richard and Catherine Kroeger has argued convincingly that it was especially the cult of Dionysus that was popular in Corinth at that time and that this explains some of the problems that Paul faces with this turbulent congregation.[3] Paul complains of drunkenness at the Eucharist, and drinking sessions were an important part of the Dionysiac cult. We gather from Paul's letter that Christians went on attending pagan feasts, and presumably Dionysiac revels. Pausanias tells that there were two statues of Dionysus in the Agora, and so he must have been a popular figure.[4] One of the characteristics of a good Dionysiac session was the wild screaming and yelling of the women, the *ololugmos* or *ololugma*. If the Corinthian women had come to think that this was all part of a proper religious celebration then it would explain why eucharists at Corinth were quite so chaotic, with

everyone yelling in tongues. The Kroegers argue that when Paul
tells the women that they must keep quiet in church he is not
consigning them to silence since he has already accepted that they
can pray and prophesy. They suggest, though this is arguable, that
lalein here does not have its ordinary meaning, 'to speak', but 'to
make a row':

> During the classical age *lalein* often applied to the making of noise
> which had no significant meaning. Indeed, it is essentially an
> onomatopoeic word embodying 'la-la', often a ritual cry of the
> *clamor*. The Bacchic 'Eleleu' also involved the reduplicated 'l'
> sound, a phenomenon still employed by ululating women of
> Turkey, Iran, Sephardic Jewry, Tanzania and the American
> charismatic movement.[5]

One of the characteristics of the cult of Dionysus was a fascination
with the reversal of sexual identities; men dressed up as women
and women as men. Increasingly the god was portrayed as being
effeminate; he was called 'the sham man', 'male-female', 'double-
natured'.[6] He was the god who upset the ordinary distinctions of
this world in his mad freedom, the god of *akatastasias*, of 'upside-
downing', the liberator of women whom he had 'driven from the
shuttle and the loom.'[7] But Paul warns his congregation that 'God
is not a God of confusion [*akatastasias*], but of peace' (14.33). This
suggests a plausible context in which Paul would have had to ask
some hard-headed questions about the relationship between sexual
identity and Christian identity, between nature and grace. Is the
rejection of gender identity a sign of one's freedom in Christ or
of contempt for God's creation?

Paul starts by referring to the tradition he passed on to the
Corinthians:

> I commend you because you remember me in everything and
> maintain the traditions even as I have delivered them to you
> (11.2).

He begins, then, by reminding the Corinthians that they belong
within the wider family of the Church. When he closes the debate

in 11.16 he returns to the same point: 'If anyone is disposed to be contentious, we recognize no other practice, nor do the churches of God.' The reason that Paul appeals to the received tradition, at this and other moments of his argument, is not that he is a hidebound traditionalist. Traditions were what joined you to your origins, in this case the Jerusalem Church, and for a first-century Jew to ask what something was, was to ask about its origins. Just as in the Old Testament one explored what it meant to be a human being by telling the story of Adam and Eve, so one asked what it meant to be a Christian by understanding the origins. There was no abstract Hebrew conception of 'nature'; one told the story of the beginnings and discovered how one related to them. The problem that faced these Corinthians was that as redeemed women and men they could locate their identity by reference to two stories, the story of creation, and the story of Christ, but what was the relationship between the two? Does the story of Christ supersede, make redundant, the story of creation? How do the narratives relate? That is the way in which the question of the relationship between nature and grace is first posed.

Paul continues:

> But I want you to understand that the head of every man is Christ, the head of a woman is her husband, and the head of Christ is God. (11.3)

Jerome Murphy O'Connor has argued that the word translated by 'head' here (*kephalē*) cannot have the meaning of 'authority'.[8] In the Septuagint (LXX), the Greek translation of the Old Testament, it is almost never used in this sense. It can have either its literal sense of that which is on top of one's shoulders, or else it can mean the source or origin of something, as when a spring is said to be the *kephalē* of a river. The Hebrew word *Rosh* can mean either a head, in the literal sense of the word, or someone who bears authority, like the head of a tribe, but when it has the latter meaning it is virtually never translated by *kephalē*. There is simply no basis for the assumption that a Hellenised Jew would instinctively give *kephalē* the meaning 'one having authority over someone.'[9] The RSV translation also sends us off in the wrong direction by giving

After Eve

us: 'the head of a woman is her husband'. If one's assumption is that the text is about the subordination of women to men then that is a perfectly natural interpretation. To what other man would a woman be subject? But what the text actually says is something quite different: the source of a woman is man. It has nothing to do with authority; Paul is taking us back to the story of Genesis and reminding us that in the beginning woman was made from the man's rib. Faced with these Corinthians who believe that they have transcended gender distinctions, who glorify in their freedom in Christ by dressing up in each other's clothes, Paul points us back to the story of Creation to establish what it means to have a male or female nature. His argument is that there was from the beginning, prior to sin, a distinction between the sexes. Being male or female is not a symptom of being fallen.

It is less clear what Paul means by saying that 'the head of every man is Christ'. I believe that in this context this must also refer to the story of Creation.[10] It is generally accepted that Paul believed in the pre-existence of Christ. In 8.6 he had written: 'For us there is one God, the Father, from whom are all things and for whom we exist, and one Lord, Jesus Christ, through whom are all things, and through whom we exist.' So this statement that 'the head of every man is Christ' probably points us back to Christ who is the source both of our natural existence and of our redemption. There can be no contradiction between nature and grace. Both ultimately derive from God, who is the source of all that is.

The argument continues to unfold in the next couple of verses:

Any man who prays or prophesies with head covered dishonours his head, but any woman who prays or prophesies with her head unveiled dishonours her head – it is the same as if her head were shaven (11.4–5).

These verses may appear too much for even the most valiant Pauline apologist, but Murphy O'Connor has shown us a way forward. He has demonstrated that there is, in fact, no reference to either hats or veils in this passage.[11] They have only been introduced into translation to explain a complex Greek text. Take the text, 'Any man who prays or prophesies with his head covered dishonours his head'. The Greek (*Kata kephalēs echōn*) means 'having something hanging from his head'. Paul cannot have believed that it was dishonourable for a man to have his head covered in church. As a Jew he grew up in a culture in which priests had turbans on their heads and it is possible that the custom of men covering their heads with prayer shawls was already established. It is far more probable that he is referring to men having long hair. Jews and Greeks wore their hair short in the first century and long hair would have been considered a sign of effeminacy. This interpretation is confirmed by verse 14: 'Does not nature itself teach you that for a man to wear long hair is degrading to him?' For a man to wear long hair, and especially hair bound up in coils and buns, was for him to deny his maleness, flouting the marks of gender differentiation. It was a common topic at the time. Pseudo-Phocylides gets quite carried away on the subject. 'If a child is a boy, do not let locks grow on his head. Braid not his crown nor make crossknots on his head. Long hair is not fit for men, but for voluptuous women. Guard the youthful beauty of a comely boy, because many rage for intercourse with a man.'[12]

Part of the interest of this passage by Paul is that here we can see two ways of talking about nature meeting and becoming entangled with each other. On the one hand there is the Jewish tradition of exploring something's nature by telling stories of its origins, which is why Paul takes us back to Genesis. But we can also detect echoes of a Stoic understanding of nature, as in verse 14, 'Does not nature itself teach you that for a man to wear long hair is degrading to him?' Here Paul is much closer to Epictetus, who could be quite lyrical on the educational value of beards:

Can anything be more useless than the hairs on a chin? Well, what then? Has not nature used even these in the most suitable way possible? Has she not by these means distinguished between the male and the female? Does not the nature of each one among us cry aloud forthwith from afar, 'I am a man; on this understanding approach me, on this understanding talk with me; ask for nothing further; behold the signs'? Again, in the case of women, just as nature has mingled in their voice a certain softer note, so likewise she has taken hair from their chins. [Not, you

notice, added it to male chins.] Not so, you say: on the contrary
the human animal ought to have been left without distinguishing
features, and each of us ought to proclaim by word of mouth,
'I am a man'. Nay, but how fair and becoming and dignified
the sign is! How much fairer than the cock's comb. How much
more magnificent than the lion's mane. Wherefore we ought to
preserve the signs that God has given; we ought not to throw
them away; we ought not, so far as in us lies, to confuse the sexes
which have been distinguished in this fashion.[13]

Part of the complexity of teasing out the relationship between
nature and grace is that Paul's text is marked by a tension between
two conceptions of nature, of a 'nature itself' that teaches, and of
nature as disclosed and explored in the dynamics of a narrative.

Paul is no more concerned to put hats on women than he is to
remove them from men. The word which is translated by the RSV
as 'unveiled' in verse 5 – 'any woman who prays or prophesies
with her head unveiled dishonours her head' – need not necessarily
mean that at all. *Akatakaluptos* certainly can mean 'uncovered' but,
according to Murphy O'Connor, it can have the meaning of
'disordered' or 'unbound'. And this is clearly how Paul wishes the
word to be taken here. It would be very odd if in verse 5 he were
to be insisting on women wearing veils and then in verse 15 telling
the Corinthians that it is precisely the women's hair that is given
to her for a covering. That would appear to make veils rather
redundant! So it seems that these Corinthian women were
disregarding convention and letting their hair hang loose, unbound.
And why this might have been an appealing thing to do is explained,
once again, by the practices of the mystery cults. Wild, unbound
hair was a sign of protest against oppression, of freedom from the
loom and the household. The Kroegers write, 'Dishevelled hair and
head thrown back were almost trademarks of the maenads in Greek
vase painting and in literary sources. The wild tossing head was
also a distinctive of Cybele worshippers, and often the locks which
had been so frantically whipped about were shorn off as a sacrifice
to the goddess.'[14] If the more frenetic cult devotees were inclined
to cut off their locks, then this would explain Paul's apparent *non
sequitur* in verse 5, that if women are going around with unbound

hair then they might as well shave their heads. If you want to be like one of these followers of the cult, then why not go the whole way? But the Corinthians saw it as a celebration of their freedom in Christ. They had passed beyond the fallen world of gender differentiation. This was all of a piece with their tolerance of the man whom Paul condemns for committing incest with his stepmother (5.1). Murphy O'Connor wrote:

> If there was no longer any male or female, the Corinthians felt free to blur the distinctions between the sexes. Unmasculine and unfeminine hairdos flew in the face of accepted conventions in precisely the same way as their approval of incest. Scandal was the symbol of their new spiritual freedom; the more people they shocked, the more right they felt themselves to be.[15]

Paul says that men and women who behave in this way 'dishonour their heads'. I suspect that there may be a subtle pun here. They not only dishonour their heads in the literal sense of the word, but also in the sense of their source, the one from whom they come. They are denying their origins and thus their proper natures. And this is the same line of thought which lies behind the next two verses:

> For a man ought not to adopt a feminine hairstyle, since he is the image and glory of God; but woman is the glory of man. For man was not made from woman, but woman from man. Neither was man created for woman, but woman for man (11.7–8).

Once again Paul is referring us back to Genesis. I take it that the word 'glory' (*doxa*) here means something like 'radiance' or 'reflection'. Man is the glory of God in the sense that he points us back to the one from whom he comes, his creator, just as the light points us back to the light bulb. Similarly, to say that woman is the glory of man is not to say that Mrs Jones is Mr Jones's proudest possession, but rather that the existence of women points us back to the stories of the beginning, when God made man from the earth and then made woman from man. Our stories tell us of a difference that precedes the Fall. The trouble is that Paul then seems to deduce from that a subordination, 'neither was man created for woman, but woman for man'. Now it is perfectly true that this is what Genesis 2 says. The question, to which we shall return, is whether in the light of Christ we do not have to retell the story of our origins. Does grace transform our perception of nature? The stories of Genesis now find themselves in a new context, a canon that includes the Christ in whom there is neither male nor female. And Paul now takes us into this larger context in the next verses. The RSV translation reads:

> That is why a woman ought to have a veil on her head, because of the angels. Nevertheless, in the Lord woman is not independent of man, or man of woman, for as woman was made from man, so man is now born of woman, and all things are from God (11.10–12).

There is, of course, not a hint of a hat in the Greek text. The reference to veils was introduced, presumably, to explain an otherwise obscure text. The Greek reads, 'That is why a woman ought to have authority on her head, because of the angels.' A popular explanation has been that a veil would have been necessary to prevent the angels from seeing her beauty and lusting after her. In Genesis 6 the sons of God had gazed on the daughters of men and slept with them, thus overthrowing the proper order of creation and bringing about the Flood. But I do not think that this is what Paul has in mind here. In first-century Judaism the angels were seen as the guardians of creation, celestial bureaucrats who made sure that chaos did not overwhelm the world. They were entrusted with making sure that everything functioned according to God's plan. Women pretending to be men would have been deeply offensive to these tidy-minded spirits. So Paul is probably asserting that women have authority in the Church not by transcending their sexuality, but in virtue of it, as women. Their hair is a sign of who they are, their nature, and therefore that in virtue of which they exercise authority in the Church. And it is certain that in Paul's Church many women did exercise considerable influence. 'In the Lord' the subordination implied by the Genesis story is transcended by the mutuality of the life of grace, for in Christ 'woman is not independent of man, or man of woman'. And this graced mutuality is confirmed by the fact of nature that now man is born of woman just as woman came from man.

One could conclude by saying that the fundamental principle that Paul is asserting here is clearly important. Whatever grace does it does not destroy nature. We find Paul at the beginning of a long theological tradition that leads to Aquinas' dictum that '*gratia non tollat naturam sed perficiat*' [grace does not scrap nature but brings it to perfection].[16] The Corinthian rejection of sexual differentiation leads, in the end, to a denial of the goodness of God's creation, dualism, Marcionism, Gnosticism and all manner of horrible things. That the story of Christ embraces and brings to its proper conclusion the story of our creation is surely right and proper. But there are still problems in how one should relate nature and grace which Paul has not solved. The stories of the origins, the founding myths of Genesis, imply a subordination of woman to man that we would not wish to accept as natural, of the order of nature. But given the theological and narrative tradition within which Paul grew up, how else could he have talked about our created natures? Perhaps one could argue that if grace perfects nature and discloses its deepest potentialities, then it is only in Christ that we discover what our nature is. The mutuality of life 'in the Lord', in whom there is neither male nor female, must suggest that it is mutuality for which we are made. It is not finally the case that grace replaces a natural subordination with an equality. What is at issue is how one relates the stories of Genesis to the story of Christ, and already in Paul, with his theology of the pre-existent Christ who shared in the Father's work of creation, we have an important hint that the story of Christ in some sense embraces and transforms the story of the origins. It is the incarnate Son of God who finally discloses who we are and for what we are made. It is only our life in Christ that finally reveals what it means for us to be male or female.

We may imagine naively that sexual identity is just a matter of biology, a merely physical fact about us. But if we place this in the wider context of 1 Corinthians and Paul's extended meditation on what it means to be bodily, then it is seen to be more. For Paul to be bodily is to be able to be present to someone; it is to be able

72

to give oneself away. This is what lies behind his sexual ethics, his understanding of the Eucharist as the meal in which Christ gives us himself, his theology of the Church as the body of Christ, and his doctrine of the resurrection of the body. The human body is not just a bag of flesh and bones but the possibility of self-gift and mutual presence.[17] So what is at issue in one's sexual identity is not just a matter of anatomy, but the possibility of presence to another person. So one might suggest it is only grace, life in Christ, that can ultimately disclose what it means to be female or male. It is only the slow process of healing one's nature from the effects of sin and egoism and injustice that will enable us to discover what it means to be a man or a woman.

NOTES

1. Dominique Stein, '*Le statut des femmes dans les lettres de Paul*', *Lumière et Vie*, Vol. 139, Septembre–Octobre 1978, pp. 63–86.
2. Cf. Timothy Radcliffe OP, '"Glorify God in your bodies": A Pauline basis for sexual ethics', *New Blackfriars*, July/August 1986, pp. 306–14.
3. Richard and Catherine Kroeger, 'An Inquiry into the evidence of Maenadism in the Corinthian Congregation', *Society of Biblical Literature 1978 Seminar Papers*, Vol.2 ed. P.J. Achtemeier, pp. 331–8.
4. *Description of Greece*, 2.6.
5. Kroeger, op. cit., p. 335.
6. Ibid., p. 333.
7. Euripides, *The Bacchae*, 119.
8. 'Sex and Logic in 1 Corinthians 11.2–16', *The Catholic Biblical Quarterly*, Vol. 42, October 1980, pp. 482–500.
9. Ibid., p. 492.
10. Murphy O'Connor gives an alternative but, I believe, less plausible interpretation of this verse.
11. Op. cit., pp. 483ff.
12. P.W. van de Horst, *The Sentences of Pseudo-Phocylides with Introduction and Commentary* (SVTP 4; Leiden, Brill, 1978), pp. 81–3, vv. 210–14.
13. Dis. 1.16.9–14.
14. Op. cit., p. 332.
15. Op. cit., p. 490.
16. *Summa Theologica*, 1.q.1.a.2.ad.2.
17. Cf. Radcliffe, op. cit., p. 308.

5

The Holy Spirit as Feminine in Early Syriac Literature

Sebastian Brock

In his Commentary on Isaiah[1] Jerome quotes from a passage in the Gospel according to the Hebrews where Jesus proclaims that 'my mother the Holy Spirit has taken me . . . [and conveyed me to Mount Tabor]'. No one should be scandalised on this matter, comments Jerome, in that 'Spirit' is feminine in Hebrew, but masculine in 'our language' (Latin) and neuter in Greek, 'for in the deity there is no gender' [*in divinitate enim nullus est sexus*]. The aim of this paper is to explore some of the repercussions of this grammatical feature of the Semitic languages in the history of the only early Christian literature to have been written in one of these languages, namely Syriac.

Although the New Testament was written in Greek, Christianity was born in a Semitic milieu and Jesus himself will have spoken Aramaic (of which Syriac is a dialect). Likewise, in those parts of the eastern Roman Empire where Aramaic, rather than Greek, was both spoken and written (such as much of Syria and Palestine), Aramaic became the language of many early Christian communities; accordingly, when these communities spoke of the Holy Spirit they naturally used the standard Aramaic word for 'spirit', *ruḥa* (also 'wind' as *pneuma*), which, like Hebrew *ruaḥ*, is grammatically feminine. Thus, when referring to the Holy Spirit, they used the feminine forms of adjectives, verbs, etc. What effect does this purely grammatical feature have on their understanding of the role of the Holy Spirit? In what way does it affect the images and metaphors they use of the Spirit? In particular is the image of the Holy Spirit as 'mother' found elsewhere, as well as in the Gospel according to the Hebrews?

Before turning to the evidence of Syriac literature we should briefly look at the role of grammatical gender in different languages, for it is important to realise that differences in this role will give rise to different sensitivities. For our present purpose it will suffice to notice five different possibilities.

(1) In English there are separate pronouns, 'he', 'she', 'it', but no special feminine forms for the article, for adjectives or for verbs. Gender is thus mostly confined to persons.

(2) French has only the masculine and feminine pronouns, but it also has separate feminine forms for the article and adjectives. Thus, for example, l'Esprit is grammatically masculine. Gender affects things as well as persons.

(3) The situation in Greek is similar to that in French, except that there are three separate pronouns. Thus *to pneuma to hagion* is neuter.

(4) In Hebrew, Aramaic and Syriac, while there are only two pronouns, masculine and feminine, separate feminine forms exist for verbs as well as for adjectives (but not for the article).

(5) In certain languages, such as Armenian, no grammatical gender exists and a single pronoun covers both 'he' and 'she'. Revisers of modern liturgies and biblical translations will lament that the English language does not have this simple solution to the problem of 'sexist language'.

This difference in the role played by grammatical gender in different languages means that we should not necessarily think that the surprise which we may feel if we hear the Holy Spirit described as 'she' would have also been felt in a language where the word for 'spirit' is feminine anyway.

With these preliminaries let us turn to see what happens in the literature of the Syriac-speaking Church. First of all, it is important to look at these texts in historical perspective, for over the course of time practice can be observed to change. Three stages can be identified:

(1) In the earliest literature up to about AD 400 the Holy Spirit is virtually always treated grammatically as feminine. This is the norm in the three main monuments of early Syriac literature, the Acts of Thomas, and the writings of Aphrahat and Ephrem.

(2) From the early fifth century onwards it is evident that some people began to disapprove of treating the Holy Spirit as grammatically feminine; accordingly, in defiance of the grammatical rules of the language, they treated the word *ruḥa* as masculine wherever it referred to the Holy Spirit. Perhaps this shift in practice was in part due to the ever increasing prestige of the Greek language (though of course *pneuma* is neuter, rather than masculine).

(3) From the sixth century onwards what had been only sporadic practice in the fifth century now becomes the norm, *ruḥa,* referring to the Holy Spirit, is regularly treated as masculine. Even so, the original feminine was not completely ousted, for it can still occasionally be found, chiefly in liturgical texts and in poetry (where some poets use either masculine or feminine, depending on which best fits their immediate metrical requirements).

This three-stage development happens to be neatly reflected in the history of the biblical translations into Syriac. Thus in the Old Syriac translation of the Gospels, dating from the late second or early third century, the Holy Spirit regularly features grammatically as feminine. In the revised translation of the Syriac New Testament, known as the Peshitta, and produced in the early fifth century, we find that although the feminine has been preserved in many places, there are also some where the gender has been altered to masculine. Finally, in the early seventh-century version known as the Harklean (a masterpiece of mirror translation) *ruḥa* is regularly treated as masculine wherever it refers to the Holy Spirit. It is likely that this practice was also adopted in the Philoxenian revision of 507/8, now lost apart from quotations.

These developments may be illustrated by means of some examples, beginning with the Syriac Bible.

Rather surprisingly there are only two places in the Gospels where the revisers who produced the Peshitta chose to alter the feminine of the Old Syriac to masculine; it so happens that both are passages where the Holy Spirit 'teaches' (Luke 12.12 and John 14.26). Much more frequently in the Gospels the Peshitta simply retains the feminine of the Old Syriac; this includes two contexts of central importance, the Annunciation (Luke 1.35) and the Baptism.[2] It is, curiously, in Acts that the Peshitta provides the highest number of cases where a masculine form is used in connection with the Holy

Spirit (nine instances),[3] but even in that book the feminine survives in a further seven passages.[4] There appears to be no clear rationale behind this variation in usage. In the Peshitta of the Epistles, on the other hand, the archaic usage with the feminine is kept throughout.[5]

The only consistent alteration made by the Peshitta revisers (and this is confined to the Gospels) concerns the precise Syriac terminology for the Holy Spirit. Although the Old Syriac normally employs the phrase 'Spirit of holiness', *ruha d-qudsha*, of Jewish origin,[6] in five passages[7] it uses instead the feminine adjective, *ruha qaddishta*, 'Holy Spirit'; all five of these the Peshitta alters to *ruha d-qudsha*, though the feminine is retained in the single case (Luke 2.25) where the context does not leave the gender indeterminate. This situation is quite different from that in the Peshitta Epistles, where *ruha qaddishta* is to be found at Eph. 4:30 and 1 Thess. 4:8. It comes as no surprise to find that the form with the masculine adjective, *ruha qaddisha*, occurs only in the post-Peshitta version of the minor Catholic Epistles known as the *Pococke Epistles* (early sixth century?), and in the Harklean New Testament.[8]

The alteration to masculine of biblical passages which originally had feminine can also take place at a subsequent stage, either in the manuscript tradition of the Syriac Bible, or in quotations by later writers. Two examples will suffice. In the much used Psalm 51 the original Peshitta text has the feminine adjective in verse 13, 'Take not thy Holy Spirit, *ruhak qaddishta*, from me'; this is preserved only in a few of the oldest manuscripts,[9] and the alteration to masculine *qaddisha* is already found in the earliest complete Syriac Bible, *Codex Ambrosianus*, of the six/seventh century. Another important verse is 1 Cor. 3.16, where the Peshitta uses the feminine: 'The Spirit of God dwells (*'amra*, feminine) in you'. The great Syrian Orthodox theologian Philoxenus (died 523) alters the verb to the masculine (*'amar*) when he quotes the passage;[10] the same phenomenon can be observed when he quotes other key New Testament passages referring to the activity of the Spirit, such as Luke 1.35;[11] it is thus likely that the (lost) Philoxenian revision of the Syriac New Testament regularly removed usage with the feminine, anticipating the Harklean's practice. The same phenomenon can be observed in the transmission of Christian

Palestinian Aramaic biblical texts. In this version (of uncertain date, possibly fifth century) the feminine is the norm, but at Luke 3.22, for example, some manuscripts have altered the verb to masculine.

Before turning to non-biblical literature one further analogous feature of the Syriac Gospels should be mentioned. In Syriac *Logos*, 'Word', is translated by another feminine noun, *mellta*. Accordingly in the Prologue of the Gospel of John the Old Syriac treats *Mellta*, the Logos, as feminine, and this usage is reflected, not only in the fourth-century writer Ephrem (which is to be expected);[12] but also very occasionally in texts of the fifth, or even later centuries,[13] even though in the Peshitta revision the gender had already been altered to masculine.

In the non-biblical literature of the earliest of the three periods outlined above it is very exceptional to find cases where the Holy Spirit is treated grammatically as masculine. Curiously enough the one text where the masculine adjective (*ruḥa*) *qaddisha* does occur several times is the archaic *Odes of Solomon*,[14] but this is not the place to try to explain this surprising state of affairs. Otherwise the only other occurrences of usage with masculine are a few passages in the hymns of Ephrem[15] (who otherwise regularly employs the feminine). It should be added that usage with feminine is also the norm in early translations into Syriac from Greek (e.g. Eusebius, *Theophania, Ecclesiastical History, Palestinian Martyrs*).

The fifth century is clearly the period of transition, and it would be of interest to trace in detail the development of usage over the course of the century in different texts. This task remains to be done, but my general impression is that it is those writers who are more theologically aware (aware, that is, of contemporary controversies) who are more likely to employ the masculine. Thus, towards the end of the century, both Narsai (in the Antiochene christological tradition) and Philoxenus (in the Alexandrine) use the masculine, while the author of the Life of Symeon the Stylite still employs the feminine.[16] The great poet Jacob of Serugh (died 521) happily uses both feminine and masculine, indifferently.[17]

From the sixth century onwards usage with the masculine (and normally with *ruḥa qaddisha*, rather than *ruḥa d-qudsha*) appears to be invariable in theological writing, and it is only sporadically in poetry that the feminine is still to be found (many examples – still in liturgical use – can be gathered from the pages of the *Fenqitho* and *Ḥudra*, the Festal Hymnaries of the Syrian Orthodox Church and the Church of the East).

Thus far we have solely been concerned with surface phenomena connected with the grammatical structure of the language. Does this fact that the Holy Spirit is grammatically feminine in the earliest Syriac literature have any effect on the way people envisaged the role of the Spirit? That it did is suggested by a passage in the Gospel according to Philip, a work preserved only in Coptic (among the Nag Hammadi finds) but probably having a Syrian background; here, at §17 we find: 'Some have said, "Mary conceived of the Holy Spirit". They are wrong . . . when did a woman ever conceive of a woman?' Passages implying that the Spirit acts in a male role as the source of Mary's conception can be found in some later liturgical texts, such as the following, where Gabriel addresses Mary: 'You shall discover a wonderful conception: without [human] seed or intercourse, your conception shall be from the Holy Spirit, O Virgin.'[18] It was perhaps in order to obviate such a literalist reading of Luke 1.35 that many later Syriac writers deliberately distinguish between the 'Holy Spirit' and the 'Power of the Most High' in that verse, identifying the Power (*ḥayla*, masculine in Syriac) as the Logos.[19]

The author of the Gospel according to Philip clearly sees the Spirit as female, and it is this, evidently Semitic, tradition that is represented in a number of early Syriac works where we encounter the Spirit as Mother.[20] The Acts of Thomas, perhaps of the third century, is the earliest of these. This work, whose original language was Syriac (this is now generally agreed), survives in a re-worked Syriac form and in a Greek translation which was made from a more primitive form of the Syriac original. Thus, in the course of several prayers uttered by Judas Thomas, the Greek text includes several invocations to the Holy Spirit as 'Mother'; in the surviving Syriac, however, this term is always absent, presumably having been removed on the grounds that it was no longer considered appropriate. The relevant passages in the Greek text are as follows:[21]

§27 [In a baptismal context; the invocation is addressed to both the Son and the Spirit.] Come, holy name of Christ, which is above every name; come Power of the Most High, and perfect mercy; come exalted gift [i.e. the Holy Spirit]; come, compassionate mother . . . [For 'compassionate mother' the Syriac has nothing corresponding.]

§50 [An invocation to the Spirit in the context of the Eucharist.] . . . Come, hidden mother . . . come, and make us share in this Eucharist which we perform in your name, and [make us share] in the love to which we are joined by invoking you. [The Syriac again removes the reference to the Spirit as 'mother'.]

§133 [In the course of a trinitarian invocation in the context of the Eucharist.] We name over you [the newly baptised] the name of the Mother. [Syriac: the name of the Spirit.]

In one further passage, a prayer in §39, the Greek text has an intrusive 'and', wrongly separating the epithet Mother from the Holy Spirit: 'We hymn you [Christ] and your unseen Father and your Holy Spirit *and* the Mother of all created things.'[22]

In these passages we have clear evidence of a Trinity envisaged as consisting of Father, Mother and Son. Traces of this are also to be found in the archaic poem known as the Hymn of the Pearl (or, of the Soul), incorporated into the Acts of Thomas. The poem describes how a royal son was sent by his father and mother, the king and the queen, from the highlands of the East (the heavenly world) to go to Egypt (the fallen world) in order to collect a pearl from the mouth of a dragon. Although the interpretation of the poem has been much disputed,[23] a reasonable case can be made out for seeing the son as representing in some senses both Adam/humanity and Christ the Word who rescues him. In Egypt the son receives a letter from his parents which begins: 'From your Father, the King of kings, and your Mother, the Mistress of the East', and later he uses the names of his father and mother in an invocation to charm the dragon so that he can extract the pearl. In some sense or other it seems likely that the King and the Queen are to be identified as the Father and the Holy Spirit; in any case, this was the Christian reading of the poem in antiquity.

The Acts of Thomas might be considered as belonging at best only to the fringes of orthodoxy. It is not, however, the only place in early Syriac literature where we encounter the Spirit as Mother. A thoroughly orthodox witness to this tradition is Aphrahat, writing in the middle of the fourth century. Aphrahat, or the Persian Sage as he was called, lived within the Sasanid Empire, and so it is no great surprise that his theological language seems archaic when compared with that of his contemporaries writing within the Roman Empire. In a work dealing mainly with virginity he has the following interpretation of Genesis 2.24 ('a man shall leave his father and mother'):[24]

> Who is it who leaves father and mother to take a wife? The meaning is as follows: as long as a man has not taken a wife, he loves and reveres God his Father and the Holy Spirit his Mother, and he has no other love. But when a man takes a wife, then he leaves his (true) Father and his Mother.

The seeds for such an interpretation had already been sown by Philo (not that Aphrahat would have read him) in his *Allegorical Interpretation* (of Gen. 2–3). At II.49, after quoting Gen. 2.24, he says:[25]

> For the sake of sense-perception the Mind, when it has become her slave, abandons both God the Father of the universe, and God's excellence and wisdom, the Mother of all things, and cleaves to and becomes one with sense-perception and is resolved into sense-perception so that the two become one flesh and one experience.

Closer to Aphrahat in time, space and spirit, however, are the Macarian Homilies, whose Syrian/Mesopotamian origin in the fourth/fifth century is now generally admitted. Here we encounter the following passage, which again reflects Gen.2.24:[26]

> It is right and fitting, children, for you to have left all that is temporal and to have gone off to God: instead of an earthly father you are seeking the heavenly Father, and instead of a mother who is subject to corruption, you have as a Mother the excellent Spirit of God, and the heavenly Jerusalem. Instead of the brothers

you have left you now have the Lord who has allowed himself to be called brother of the faithful.

It is important to realise that the image of the Holy Spirit as Mother is by no means confined to Syriac writers or to those working in a Semitic milieu. Thus Hippolytus, writing in Greek *c*.200, describes Isaac as an image of God the Father, his wife Rebecca as an image of the Holy Spirit, and their son Jacob as an image of Christ – or of the Church.[27] Most striking in this respect, however, is the second Hymn of the highly cultured Synesios, Bishop of Cyrene from 410–13. After addressing the Father and the Son he turns to the Spirit:[28]

I sing of the [Father's] travail, the fecund will, the intermediary principle, the Holy Breath/Inspiration, the centre point of the Parent, the centre point of the Child: she is mother, she is sister, she is daughter; she has delivered [i.e. as midwife] the hidden root.

Examples of the same kind of imagery used of the Spirit can also be found in a few Latin writers, most notably in Marius Victorinus (mid fourth century).

Thus among early Christian writers, Greek and Latin as well as Syriac, one can find scattered pieces of evidence which may suggest that there was once a fairly widespread tradition which associated the Holy Spirit with the image of mother.[29] The roots of such a tradition are to be found, not only in the grammatical feature of the Semitic languages where 'Spirit' is feminine, but also in the links which the concept of Holy Spirit will have had with the personalised figure of Wisdom[30] and with the Jewish concept of the Divine Presence or Shekhina.[31] As is well known, both these features are often connected with mother imagery. As far as extant early Syriac literature is concerned, however, neither Wisdom nor the Shekhina is at all prominent.

As we have seen, from the fifth century onwards a revulsion against the idea of the Holy Spirit as mother must have set in. This may partly have been due to the misuse of the imagery by some heretical groups, though another factor should also be kept in mind:

in the Syriac-speaking areas of the eastern Roman Empire the large scale influx of new converts to Christianity will have included many people whose background lay in pagan cults in which a divine triad of Father, Mother and Son was prominent.[32]

The archaic tradition of the Holy Spirit as Mother did not, however, entirely disappear, for one can find occasional relics of it, albeit reduced to a simile, in much later Syriac writers. Thus the monastic writer Martyrius, writing in the first half of the seventh century, speaks of the person 'who has been held worthy of the hovering of the all-holy Spirit, who, like a mother, hovers over us as she gives sanctification; and through her hovering over us, we are made worthy of sonship'.[33] The term 'hovering' here will immediately have provided Syriac readers with three resonances, of which Genesis 1.2 is the primary one; more important, however, in the context within which Martyrius is speaking, are the resonances of the baptismal rite, where the Spirit 'hovers over' the font,[34] and the eucharistic epiclesis, where the Spirit is invited to come and 'hover over' the Bread and the Wine and thus transform them into the Body and the Blood of Christ.[35]

Another example of the imagery can be found in the writings of the Syrian Orthodox theologian and scholar, Moses bar Kepha (died 903): 'the Holy Spirit hovered over John the Baptist and brought him up like a compassionate mother'.[36] For the most part, however, in later Syriac literature it will be found that 'Grace' has taken over the Spirit's place as mother.[37]

Whereas the Holy Spirit as Mother, alongside God the Father, is a feature only encountered rarely in Syriac literature, the use of female imagery is much more common. Such imagery is implied, for example, every time the term 'hovers' is used of the Holy Spirit – and it occurs very frequently – for this term, based as we have seen on Genesis 1.2, originally describes the action of a mother bird. Rather than explore this aspect further here, it must suffice to observe that female imagery is by no means confined to the Holy Spirit: many examples can be found (and this applies to Greek and Latin literature, as well as Syriac) where female imagery is used of the Father and the Son. What to us seems a bizarre example can be found in the Odes of Solomon (late second century?):[38]

A cup of milk was offered to me, and I drank it in the sweetness of the Lord's kindness. The Son is the cup, and the Father is he who was milked; and the Holy Spirit is she who milked him. Because his breasts were full, and it was undesirable that his milk should be ineffectually released, the Holy Spirit opened her bosom, and mixed the milk of the two breasts of the Father.

An interesting example is provided by the Syriac translation of John 1.18, 'No one has ever seen God: the only Son, who is in the bosom of the Father, he has made him known'.[39] In order to render the Greek word *kolpos*, 'bosom', the Syriac translator employed a word which also means 'womb' (*ʿubba*); that at least some Syriac readers understood *ʿubba* in the sense of 'womb' at John 1.18 is shown by a number of passages in Ephrem's hymns, where he sets the 'womb' of the Father alongside the 'womb of Mary'. Thus in the Hymns on the Resurrection, I:7,

> The Word [fem.] of the Father came from his womb
> and put on a body in another womb:
> the Word proceeded from one womb to another –
> and chaste wombs are now filled with the Word.
> Blessed is he who has resided in us.

Ephrem happens to be a writer who is particularly fond of female imagery (even though he perhaps deliberately avoids any overt description of the Spirit as mother). Two examples will suffice here. In one of his Nativity Hymns (4.149–50) he describes the infant Christ, who sucks Mary's breast, as himself 'the living breast':

> He was lying there, sucking Mary's milk,
> yet all created things suck from his goodness.
> He is the living breast; from his life
> the dead have sucked living breath – and come to life.

Elsewhere, in the Hymns on the Church (25.18), Ephrem compares God to a wetnurse:

The Divinity is attentive to us, just as a wetnurse is to a baby, keeping back for the right time things that will benefit it,

for she knows the right time for weaning,
and when the child should be nourished with milk,
and when it should be fed with solid bread,
weighing out and providing what is beneficial to it
in accordance with the measure of its growing up.

In using female imagery of God Ephrem and other Syriac writers are simply following the lead set in the biblical writings themselves where such imagery applied to God is by no means infrequent – even though traditionally male-oriented eyes have usually been blind to this. In fact, throughout Christian tradition an undercurrent can be discerned where feminine imagery is used of God, and of the individual persons of the Trinity. Thus in the medieval West, to take but one example, besides the well known case of Dame Julian of Norwich, many instances can be found in writers like St Anselm and St Bernard.[40]

Clearly it is important to recover an awareness of, and a sensitivity to, this female imagery already present in the tradition, for it is only by regaining this sensitivity that it is possible to attain to a better appreciation of the fullness of the Godhead: by restricting ourselves to only fatherly images (or only motherly images), we will end up with a very unbalanced view of God.

At the same time it is essential, as Ephrem points out, to move beyond the metaphors with which God has 'allowed himself to be clothed' in the course of what could be described as his incarnation into human language:

If someone concentrates his attention solely
on the metaphors used of God's majesty,
he abuses and misrepresents that majesty
by means of those metaphors with which God has clothed himself
for humanity's own benefit,
and he is ungrateful to that Grace
which bent down its stature to the level of human childishness.
Although God had nothing in common with it,
he clothed himself in the likeness of humanity
in order to bring humanity to the likeness of himself.

(Hymns on Paradise 11:6)[41]

NOTES

1. On Isaiah 40.9 (Corpus Christianorum, Series Latina 73, p. 459).
2. Matt. 3.16, Luke 3.22, John 1.32 (at Mark 1.10 'dove' rather than 'Spirit' could be subject of the feminine verb). Other passages where the feminine is kept are Matt. 10.20 'speaks', Mark 1.12 'took him out', Luke 2.25 'was', 4.1 'led him', John 6.63 'who gives life', and 7.39 'was given'.
3. Acts 1.16 'foretold', 2.4 'gave', 10.19 and 11.12 'said', 19.6 'came', 20.23 'testifies and says', 20.28 'set up', 21.11 'said', 28.25 'spoke'.
4. Acts 1.8 'shall come', 8.18 'is given', 8.29 'said', 8.39 'snatched', 10.44 'overshadowed', 13.2 'said', 16.7 'permitted'.
5. Rom. 5.5 'was given', 8.9, 11 'dwells', 8.16 'testifies', 8.26 'assists, prays', 1 Cor. 2.10 'searches out', 3.16 and 6.19 'dwells', 12.11 'performs, distributes', Eph. 1.13 'is promised', 2 Tim. 1.14 'dwelt', Heb. 3.7 'said', 9.8 'indicated', 10.15 'testifies', 1 John 5.7 'testifies'.
6. Cp. H. Parzen, 'The Ruach hakodesh in Tannaitic literature', *Jewish Quarterly Review* 20 (1929/30), pp. 51–76.
7. Mark 13.11, Luke 2.25, 26; 11.13, John 20.22.
8. Several editions of the Syriac NT based on late manuscripts have altered Eph. 4.30 to masculine, *qaddisha*. In early Syriac literature *ruha d-qudsha* is the norm, but *ruha qaddishta* is also sometimes found, e.g. Acts of Thomas (ed. Wright), p. 323[10]; Aphrahat, *Dem*. VI.14, XXIII.61; Ephrem, *Hymns against Heresies* 55:5; *Liber Graduum* IX.1. The masculine *ruha qaddisha* is not found until the fifth century and later – with the surprising exception of the Odes of Solomon (see below, n. 14).
9. 6t1, 8a1*, 8t1, 10t4.5 in the notation of the critical edition, *Vetus Testamentum Syriace* II.3 (the first numeral denotes the century to which the manuscript is dated). At another important verse, Isaiah 11.2, Codex Ambrosianus (7a1) is the only manuscript to make a similar alteration to masculine.
10. E.g. *Tractatus tres de trinitate et incarnatione* (ed. Vaschalde, Corpus Scr. Chr. Orientalium, Scriptores Syri 9, p. 168[31]). An earlier writer who sometimes makes such alterations of gender in his biblical quotations is the monastic author John the Solitary (or John of Apamea; first half of fifth century), e.g. *Letters* (ed. Rignell), p. 113[9], quoting John 7.39
11. Substituting a masculine for the feminine form of the verb 'shall come': e.g. *Comm. on Prologue of John* (ed. de Halleux, C.S.C.O, Scriptures Syri 165, p. 41[2]). The same change is often made in liturgical texts, e.g. *Fenqitho* (Mosul edition), II, p. 83b, 87a, 88b, 95b, etc.
12. Excerpt on the Prologue of John, *apud* T. Lamy, *S. Ephrem Syri Hymni et Sermones*, II, col. 511; *Hymns on Resurrection* 1.7 (quoted below).

13. *Fenqitho* II, p. 65a (in a prayer which on other grounds must belong at least to *c.*7th century), p. 272b; VI, p. 107b, etc.
14. Odes of Solomon 6:7, 11:2, 14:8, 23:22 (in the older manuscript). Usage with the feminine verb (but not adjective) also occurs.
15. *Hymns on Faith* 12.6; *on Church* 45:15.
16. For Narsai, e.g. *Homily on Nativity*, line 151; *on Epiphany*, line 298 (both in *Patrologia Orientalis* 40). For Philoxenus see above, notes 10–11. Life of Symeon the Stylite: ed. Bedjan, *Acta Martyrum et Sanctorum* IV, p. 617, 'The Holy Spirit caused to be written down (*aktbat*, fem.) the resplendent deeds of the faithful . . .'
17. Metrical considerations are evidently uppermost in his choice of masc. or fem.; for an example see note 19.
18. *Fenqitho* II, p. 108b. Compare the polemic in Ephrem, *Hymns against Heresies* 55:3. Cp. also A. Orbe, *La teologia del Espiritu Santo* (Rome, 1966), pp. 69–116, 687–706.
19. Cf. my remarks in *Novum Testamentum* 24 (1982), p. 227, and further in *A. Guillaumont Mélanges* (Geneva, 1988) pp. 121ff. Jacob of Serugh explains the different roles of the Spirit and the Power as follows: 'The Spirit of Holiness first sanctified [fem. form of verb] her, and then [the Son of God] tabernacled in her. The Spirit freed [masc. verb] her from that debt [*or* sin], so that she might be above any wrongdoing when [the Son of God] resided in her in holy fashion' (Homily on Virgin, *apud* P. Bedjan, *Sancti Martyrii qui et Sahdona quae supersunt omnia* (Paris/Leipzig, 1902), p. 632.
20. On this see especially R. Murray, *Symbols of Church and Kingdom: a Study in Early Syriac Tradition* (Cambridge, 1975), pp. 312–20, W. Cramer, *Der Geist Gottes und des Menschen in frühsyrischer Theologie* (Münster, 1979), pp. 36–8, 68–9, and my *The Holy Spirit in the Syrian Baptismal Tradition* (Syrian Churches Series 9, 1979), pp. 3–5.
21. For §27 and §50 there is a detailed study by H. Kruse, 'Zwei Geist-Epiklesen der syrischen Thomasakten', *Oriens Christianus* 69 (1985), pp. 33–55.
22. For 'mother' the Syriac has 'hovering over' (based on Gen. 1.2, on which see below).
23. A helpful survey is provided by P-H. Poirier, *L'Hymne de la Perle des Actes de Thomas* (Louvain la Neuve, 1981).
24. *Demonstration* 18:10.
25. Translation by G.H. Whitaker (Loeb edition, p. 255).
26. Homily LIV.4.5 in H. Berthold, *Makarios/Symeon. Reden und Briefe* (Berlin, 1973), II, pp. 156–7.
27. In H. Achelis, *Hippolytus Werke* (Leipzig, 1897), I.2, p. 54[5]. For Greek writers see S. Hirsch, *Die Vorstellung von einem weiblichen pneuma hagion* (Diss. Berlin, 1926).
28. On this passage see S. Vollenweider's excursus 'Mutter Heiliger Geist' in his *Neuplatonische und christliche Theologie bei Synesios von Kyrene*

(Göttingen, 1985), pp. 78–9 (with further bibliography on the subject).

29. A different model is provided in chapter 9 of the *Didascalia* (a Syrian product of the 3rd century): there the bishop corresponds to God the Father, 'the deacon stands in the position of Christ . . . and the deaconess in the position of the Holy Spirit'.

30. In Acts of Thomas §50 the Holy Spirit is described as 'the Wisdom of the Son'; but on the whole the figure of Wisdom is not often found in early Syriac literature.

31. The Peshitta of Chronicles introduces the term in a number of passages (e.g. 2 Chron. 6.18), and it occurs a few times in Aphrahat (*Dem.* IV.7, XVIII.4, XIX.4) and Ephrem (e.g. *Hymns on Paradise* 2:11; *on Unleavened Bread* 13.21), but it only becomes popular in rather later writers such as Jacob of Serugh, and notably in some 7th/8th century(?) texts in the East Syrian *Hudra*, on which compare my *Syriac Perspectives on Late Antiquity* (London, 1984), ch. IV, pp. 106–7.

32. Such cults are well documented from Palmyra and Hatra from a rather earlier period.

33. *Book of Perfection* I.3.13 (ed. de Halleux, C.S.C.O., Scr. Syri 86, p. 32). Martyrius is a writer who frequently retains the archaic usage, treating the Spirit as grammatically feminine.

34. On this see my *The Holy Spirit in the Syrian Baptismal Tradition* (Syrian Churches Series 9, 1979), pp. 81–4. Ancient exegetes, as well as modern translators, disputed the sense of *ruaḥ 'elohim*, 'spirit/wind of God' in Gen. 1.2.

35. Many of the Syriac anaphoras employ the term 'hover' in the wording of their epicleses. It is already used in a Eucharistic context by Ephrem (*Hymns of Faith* 10:16), even though he elsewhere states that the spirit of Gen. 1.2 is not to be identified as the Holy Spirit.

36. In a homily edited by F. Nurse in *American Journal of Semitic Languages and Literature* 26 (1909/10), p. 95.

37. E.g. Jacob of Serugh, *Homiliae Selectae* (ed. P. Bedjan), IV, p. 313 (though on p. 52 he has 'the Divinity is a compassionate mother'), *Fenqitho* III, p. 137a.

38. Odes of Solomon 19:1–4, translated by R. Murray, *Symbols of Church and Kingdom*, p. 315. Similar imagery can be found especially in Clement of Alexandria; a collection of references can be found in H.J.W. Drijvers, 'The 19th Ode of Solomon', *Journal of Theological Studies* 31 (1980), pp. 344–5.

39. The following is based on my *The Luminous Eye: the Spiritual World Vision of St Ephrem* (Rome, 1985), pp. 143–4. (Ephrem's writings suggest that he had a special sympathy for women.)

40. See especially C. Bynum, *Jesus as Mother. Studies in the Spirituality of the High Middle Ages* (Berkeley, 1982).

41. English translations of several early Syriac writings are available. Odes of Solomon: in H.F.D. Sparks (ed.), *The Apocryphal Old Testament*

After Eve

(Oxford, 1984), pp. 683–731. Acts of Thomas: A.F.J. Klijn, *The Acts of Thomas* (Leiden, 1962). Aphrahat: J. Gwynn (ed.), in *A Select Library of Nicene and Post-Nicene Fathers*, II.13 (Oxford/New York, 1898), and J. Neusner, *Aphrahat and Judaism* (Leiden, 1971). Ephrem: J.B. Morris, *Select Works of St Ephrem the Syrian* (Oxford, 1847), J. Gwynn, op. cit., S.P. Brock, *The Harp of the Spirit: 18 Poems of St Ephrem* (London, 1983), and K. McVey, *Ephrem the Syrian: Hymns*, Classics of Western Spirituality (New York, 1989).

6

The Influence of Saint Jerome on Medieval Attitudes to Women

Jane Barr

It must be acknowledged at the outset that Jerome's attitudes to women accorded, on the whole, with those of earlier Church Fathers. Much of his anti-feminist propaganda was not original. What makes Jerome of supreme importance is that it was *his* writings that were read so widely, *his* opinions that were quoted and repeated throughout the succeeding centuries. Also Jerome brought to his thinking about women his own particular personal attitudes, which combined a great need of women's company, and affection for women, with a fear and hatred of their sexuality. Jerome's highly complicated personality on the one hand, and his immense erudition on the other present us with a fascinating study. Within the bounds of one essay it is possible only to select certain aspects and deal with them briefly.

In what we know of Jerome's childhood and youth there is little to help us in our understanding of the evolution of his ideas about women. Jerome wrote a large volume of letters, and it is perhaps surprising that he says so little about his parents. We know that he was born to Christian parents who were sufficiently wealthy to provide him with a good education. He does appear to have observed with care and appreciation the tenderness of mother for child, because in one of his letters, urging the duty to love one's mother, he writes: 'She put up with your bad behaviour in childhood, she washed your clothes, after getting herself messed up with excrement; she sat by your bed when you were sick.' One can perhaps discern in his reference to excrement a reflection of his extreme distaste for bodily functions, which came to be so marked in his detestation of the appearance of pregnant women. We know that he had a grandmother of whom he was fond, an aunt with whom he quarrelled, and a brother and sister much younger than himself.

After attending local schools Jerome was sent to Rome where he studied under a well-known grammarian. This is very important for Jerome's future. His great strength in his scholarship would be based on grammatical and linguistic knowledge. We know that by this time he was already assembling a considerable library. He then proceeded to rhetorical school, and followed up his formal education with a bit of travel, to Trier where he may have first encountered and become interested in monasticism. It has been suggested that Jerome's later asceticism was his reaction to an ill-spent youth. There is not much evidence for this, but Jerome does hint of scandalous behaviour in his youth, and, in insisting that virginity is the only noble state, he says he is urging the preservation of something that he himself has lost.

The next important stage in his life was his departure for the Middle East in 374 (when he was in his thirties). First came his famous dream in Antioch, in which God punished him severely for being too attached to Roman literature, and he swore an oath to God that he would never again possess or read worldly books. He did not live up to his promises (Jerome was notoriously inconsistent) and was particularly ready to quote from the Roman poets when he needed some anti-feminist ammunition.

After this he went into the Syrian desert to practise the life of a desert hermit, a stage of his life much depicted in art. Jerome spent about three years in the desert, studying, mortifying the flesh, learning Hebrew to prevent his mind being filled with erotic fantasies. (He tells us that his mind boiled with lust in the desert and he was much troubled with visions of dancing-girls.) To his disappointment he found that the desert-hermits were less saintly than he had expected, and, not by any means for the first time, or indeed the last, he quarrelled with those around him, and gave up desert-life in disgust.

After a period of study in Constantinople he went to Rome and spent the next three years there. These were at first very happy and profitable years. Jerome became deeply involved in the religious life of Rome, the Pope took a great interest in his work, he started on a new translation of the Bible (our Vulgate) and, very important for our subject, he became very friendly with a group of well-born Roman matrons. These ladies had already become very interested in asceticism, and when Jerome, with his own recent desert experience, arrived and became known to them, they hailed him with joy, and their delight was reciprocated. They met frequently for prayer and Bible study. They exchanged letters constantly on matters of Biblical exegesis and meanings of Hebrew words. This intimacy gave rise to prurient gossip. There were accusations of sexual impropriety, which Jerome hotly denied, and there was indignation that these ladies, with their high social standing, their beautiful villas on the Aventine Hill, were following a regime which involved dressing in rags, never bathing, and indeed carrying mortification of the flesh to such lengths that one young woman died.

After only three years in Rome, Jerome, unhappy and disaffected, set out for Palestine, accompanied by several of his Roman women friends, and with the aid of their considerable fortunes, he established a monastery and a convent in Bethlehem. There he lived until his death, thirty-five years later, continuing his translation and his writing, assisted by the Roman ladies, and in turn their daughters, and even a grand-daughter. There is something remarkable about the relationship between this arch-misogynist and these women. Jerome had a horror of women's sexuality. How is his attachment to them and their devotion to him reconcilable with his anti-feminist views? I think he succeeded in seeing these women, with their saintliness, their love of Scripture, their ready acceptance of asceticism, as being no longer women, but *men*. Let me quote a letter he wrote to Lucinius, a wealthy Spanish nobleman who has made a vow with his wife that they will live the rest of their married lives in complete continence. 'You have with you one who was once your partner in the flesh, but is now your partner in the spirit, once your wife but now your sister, once a woman but now a man, once an inferior but now an equal.'

Jerome constantly paints pictures of the worthlessness of a woman's life. He describes women as concerned only with their make-up, their hair, their flirtations; they are always spiteful, quarrelsome, jealous. This can be illustrated from many passages, but I select one from a letter which was picked out by E. M. Forster as the most remarkable. (E. M. Forster devoted some considerable study to St Jerome. 'That detestable father', he called him.) This was a letter addressed to a mother and daughter, who are not identified, and may well be imaginary, and it gave Jerome the opportunity to give vent to his criticisms. Addressing the young girl he goes on at length in this vein:

> The way you dress is an index of your secret desires. Your bodice is purposely ripped apart to show what is beneath, and, while hiding what is repulsive, to reveal what is beautiful. [Notice Jerome's distaste for certain parts of the female body.] You wear stays to keep your breasts in place, and confine your body in a girdle. Sometimes you let your shawl drop so as to lay bare your white shoulders . . .

Jerome's ladies, with their filthy garments, uncombed hair and never-washed bodies, certainly did not fit with such descriptions. He rejoiced, too, if they could hold their emotions in check. He tells with delight how Paula, the dearest to him of his friends, looked away firmly when her little boy held out his arms to her and her daughter wept bitterly on the quay at Ostia when she departed by ship for her new life in Bethlehem. Earlier he had reproached Paula heartlessly for grieving when another daughter died of an overdose of asceticism. He tells how Satan must rejoice at her tears. 'I miss her just as much as you do,' he says arrogantly. 'If you are a true ascetic you should be pleased to be rid of ties. Anyway, don't worry, *I* will write about her and make her immortal!'

As you see, Paula had children, indeed she had five children. How did this indulgence in sexual activity escape Jerome's condemnation? Jerome points out that she had four daughters before having a son, and that clearly she was merely facing the obligation of having to provide her husband with a son. Thus Jerome succeeded in seeing these women as separated from the weaknesses and failings of their kind, and especially from their sexuality.

During his long life Jerome wrote constantly. We have letters, commentaries on books of Scripture, long polemic articles on a variety of subjects, and, most important of all, we have his translation of the Bible. Our purpose here is to concentrate on those writings which expressed his attitudes to women. Interestingly, these are the very pieces of his work which enjoyed the greatest popularity in the thousand years after his death. When one studies the holdings of the great libraries of Europe in the Middle Ages there are almost invariably works of Jerome present, and these are most commonly the letters of Jerome concerned with women's behaviour, and the *Tract Against Jovinian* which is concerned with the necessity for virginity.

As I have said, other important figures of the early Church had written anti-feminist documents, but Jerome's writings in this field became predominant, for, I think, the following reasons.

1. Jerome was universally known and respected, particularly as translator of the Vulgate Bible. His translation was after all the chief version in use throughout the medieval world.

2. Jerome *wrote* brilliantly. The passion of his utterances, his trenchant satire, combined with the excellence of his Latin style, made his writings eminently readable. Indeed they were such models of style that they were probably sometimes read and copied for that reason alone. His writings, particularly those designed for a wider audience, are often full of stylistic and rhetorical flourishes, and these were admired and copied in certain literary circles. I have in mind the already-quoted letter to Lucinius with its successive contrasts 'Once a woman, now a man', etc.; or this – speaking of one of the devoted Roman women – 'Shut in the narrowness of a solitary cell, she enjoyed the spaciousness of Paradise.'

This leaves us with an important question. Why were the letters about women and virginity so popular? Waves of asceticism spread periodically through society in the Middle Ages. In a time of enthusiasm for asceticism, sexual activity is a particularly attractive subject for attack. A certain amount of warmth, food and shelter is needed for survival, but sex can be banned outright. This may be significant.

Jerome's greatest achievement was his translation of the Bible. (There was already a Latin Bible in existence but a new and accurate version was needed.) Jerome's Vulgate has not been traditionally regarded as a medium for the transmission of Jerome's anti-feminist views, but I think I have proved without doubt that Jerome, in his work as translator, was influenced by his prejudices, and allowed them to interfere with his accurate translation of the text. This is of course of almost unquantifiable importance. The Bible in Jerome's version was the most widely read book in the Middle Ages. Those who could not read but went to church would hear the Bible read and expounded, and if the very text of Scripture had been tampered with in any way the results could be significant.

Only two examples of Jerome's mistranslations will be cited here, because they are documented in more detail elsewhere.[1]

In the story of Joseph and Potiphar's wife in Genesis 39, where she attempts to seduce him, the original Hebrew text narrates the story in a straightforward, non-judgmental way. The woman says to Joseph 'Lie with me', and the Hebrew says simply 'and he refused'. Not so Jerome. 'And he refused' becomes 'by no means agreeing to this wicked deed'. In the course of the next few verses we have more condemnatory words introduced, for example *stuprum* which is a very strong word for vile behaviour. It is as if Jerome cannot somehow tolerate that Holy Writ does not emphasise that the woman is wicked, and feels he must do so. The quite significant changes thus made in biblical narratives are likely to have had some effect on the preaching from these texts in the medieval pulpit.

A very important alteration is made by Jerome in Genesis 3.16. God has been addressing severe words to the serpent in the garden and he finishes his warning to Eve with the words: 'Your desire will be for your husband, and he will rule over you.' While 'he will rule over you' makes clear the husband's predominance over the wife, the impact is softened somewhat by the other half of the verse, 'Your desire will be for your husband', the Hebrew word for 'desire' here having sexual content. In Jerome's version, however, that half of the verse is changed to 'You will be under the power of your husband' and 'he will rule over you' completes the verse. Complete subjection and subordination of the woman is now laid down.

This verse was much quoted, in its new form, by later writers in their exegesis of Genesis 3 and discussion of the situation of women after Eve's sin in the garden.

Only fifty years after Jerome's death we find St Eucherius of

Lyons asking the question 'If woman had not sinned, would she now be under the power of her husband [*sub potestate viri*]?' Yes, she would, he answers his own question, but it would be a subjection that operated through love. After her sin it became a servitude of fear. Almost the same words are found in the writings of Bede and Alcuin in the eighth century.

In the course of time there is a sharpening of the message. A century later we find Remigius of Auxerre adding that even against her will a woman is now subordinate to her husband. When we come to Hugh of St Victor (Paris, early twelfth century) the situation has deteriorated still further. In commenting on this verse he says: 'Not only under his rule, as before, but under his domination, so that he may afflict her with wounds.' Now, if the original mention of the woman's desire for her husband had remained in the passage, this would have changed the picture altogether.

The far-reaching effects of the change in this verse can be shown also in non-clerical literature. In the late fourteenth century a middle-aged Parisian gentleman wrote a book of instruction for his young wife. His name is unknown, and he is generally designated as 'Le Menagier de Paris', or 'the Goodman of Paris'. He was a gentle, cultivated man and his book is full of kind and thoughtful guidance, mainly concerned with the care of house and lands. It seems to me likely that the Goodman had studied the Latin of the Vulgate carefully, from certain comments he makes on Genesis stories. (He showed particular interest in stories about women.) He states firmly: 'Wives ought to be subject to their husbands as their master. So commands our God, as St Jerome says.' Then he goes on to quote Genesis 3.16 to give full and final authority to his wife's subjection.

Now let us turn to other writings of Jerome, and especially to the letters concerning women, and to the *Tract Against Jovinian*, to whose popularity I have already referred. There is so much relevant material here that it is necessary to be selective, and it will perhaps suit our purpose best if we study three particular aspects of Jerome's attitudes and influence, illustrating each of the three with examples from Jerome's writings.

Firstly let us consider Jerome's hostility to marriage, and his detestation of second marriages.

He protests that he is not against marriage. 'I praise marriage, I approve of wedlock, because they produce virgins for me.' Commenting on St Paul's statement 'It is better to marry than to burn', Jerome removes any grounds for supporting marriage from this verse by saying that this is not at all a commendation of marriage. If marriage were at all good would it be compared with burning? And to say something is better – why you could say it is better to hop about on one leg than have no legs at all!

He finds ammunition against marriage in unexpected places in the Bible.

> There is something not good in the number two . . . This we must observe, at least if we would faithfully follow the Hebrew, that while Scripture on the first, third, fourth and sixth days relates that, having finished the works of each, 'God saw that it was good', on the second day he omitted this altogether, leaving us to understand that two is not a good number because it prefigures the marriage contract. Hence it was that all the animals which Noah took into the ark in pairs were unclean. Odd numbers denote cleanness.

Here Jerome brings the poet Virgil to his aid (though he had renounced the classical writers) quoting the eighth Eclogue, 'God delights in uneven numbers.' He goes on to note that only two animals of an unclean kind were taken into the Ark (as against seven pairs of clean ones) because a second marriage is so terrible that it was not allowed even to the unclean animals.

The New Testament, too, is seen by Jerome to provide many instances of guidance on the marriage question.

For example, Jesus went only once to a marriage, thus showing that men should marry only once. John was unmarried, says Jerome, and therefore his Gospel is the most profound.

Jerome gives as the interpretation of the seed (in the gospel parable) that brings forth fruit, some a hundredfold, some sixtyfold and some ninetyfold, the following. The hundredfold which comes first represents the crown of virginity, the sixtyfold refers to widows, while the thirtyfold indicates the marriage bond. This interpretation was not original to Jerome, but the prominence he gave it helped to make it a medieval commonplace.

Jerome turns to the pagan world also to support his viewpoint. The heathens, said Jerome, placed a Virgin among the twelve signs of the Zodiac by means of which they believe the world to revolve. It is a proof of the little esteem in which they hold marriage that they did not even among the scorpions, centaurs, crabs, fishes, etc., thrust in a married couple.

Jerome's argumentation was often flawed. He was driven by the desire to convince his audience by any means he could, and he failed to see the weaknesses in his arguments. For example, when he raises a possible objection to his view on the necessity for virginity, namely that if everyone was a virgin the human race would die out, he produces sarcastic and foolish arguments. If all men were philosophers there would be no farmers, and not just farmers – there would be no lawyers or teachers. If all men were leaders, there would be no soldiers. What you are really afraid of, he says, is that if all women were virgins, there would be no prostitutes, no adulteresses. After venting all this spleen he says, quite without heat, that there is no need to worry about the future continuation of the species. Being a virgin is so hard that not many will achieve it.

Jerome more than once elaborates on the hard life of the married woman, her toils over household and children, her worries over her husband's fidelity, but one does not feel that this sincerely engages his sympathies. He detested marriage and found second marriages especially abhorrent. Here is part of his letter to a woman who is contemplating a second marriage. 'You've already learned the miseries of marriage. It's like unwholesome food, and now that you have relieved your heaving stomach of its bile, why should you return to it again like a dog to its vomit?' He enumerates various reasons why women justify second marriages. They need a father for their children. Or 'perhaps you are afraid that your noble race will die out and your father will not have a brat to crawl about his shoulders and smear his neck with filth.' Such reasons are eye-wash, says Jerome. No woman marries a man except to get him into her bed. It is the sexual activity involved in marriage that arouses his opposition.

His true feelings are also vividly expressed when he says, 'Women with child present a revolting spectacle.' 'Women soon age, and particularly if they live with men.'

The second aspect I wish to discuss and illustrate is the erotic nature of some of Jerome's writings. This is particularly obvious in what is probably the most famous letter of all, to the teenage girl Eustochium, daughter of Paula, who had already at the age of thirteen years determined on a life of chastity. He tells her he is not going to list the disadvantages of marriage, how the womb swells in pregnancy, babies wail, husbands are unfaithful and so on, thereby of course doing so. In the course of this very long letter he catalogues the sins of women, describing in detail their frivolous ways, how they dress in such a way as to hide the swelling bellies of their illicit pregnancies, and take pills to bring about abortions. How women claiming to be especially devout set up house along with priests so that they can share their devotions, but in fact share their bed. (This is a reference to the *agapetae*, a problem for the early Church.) He says that many women pretend to be pious, but think only of their bellies, and 'those parts of the body closest to their bellies'.

This, while perhaps all rather strong meat for a young girl, is none the less typical Jerome, but what is rather surprising is the extremely erotic tone of his treatment of quotations from the Song of Songs. The Song of Songs *is* an erotic document, but it was commonly interpreted at least in part in a metaphorical manner. Jerome however emphasises the erotic element. He calls Eustochium 'my lady' because she is married to our Lord, and says that her mother is the mother-in-law of God. The King, says Jerome to Eustochium, will greatly desire your beauty. He will conduct you into his bedchamber. Ever let your Bridegroom sport with you within. When sleep comes upon you he will come behind the partition and put his hand through the opening, and will touch your body, and you will arise trembling and say, 'I languish with love.' Jesus is a jealous lover.

I think we can see the effect of Jerome's sponsoring of the erotic interpretation as encouraging the adoption of the monastic life by women, and also laying the groundwork for a mystical love-literature of Jesus. Certainly the concept of Bride of Christ is made to sound less asexual than we might have expected from Jerome. But students of Jerome are accustomed to surprises.

The third point, and perhaps the most important one, is this (and here I hold Jerome responsible for a very serious disservice to women). To make his anti-feminist points more strongly, Jerome introduced pagan material, and that in a methodical manner. Now there was present in classical literature a tradition of anti-feminism. In his descriptions of women's foolish behaviour or their frivolous clothing Jerome is echoing writers like the Latin satirical poets Juvenal and Persius. But in classical writers anti-feminism was rarely formalised. Jerome's *Anti-Jovinian* set a new pattern of carefully structured and elaborated anti-feminist polemical writing.

It is a strange irony that this great saint of the Church should have preserved for us a piece of scurrilous anti-feminist writing which would otherwise have been lost, and that he should have assembled anti-feminist quotations to provide a ready ammunition for later writers. In his tirade against Jovinian (a monk who did not share Jerome's antipathy to marriage) Jerome quotes from a lost work of the Greek philosopher Theophrastus, full of vituperation against women, which would have disappeared into obscurity without Jerome's citation, but, thanks to Jerome, reached a wide audience. As well as quoting from Theophrastus at length he selects choice sentences from classical authors, for example the remark quoted by Herodotus that when a woman takes off her clothes she sheds her modesty along with them. After telling how the Romans and Greeks admired chastity, naming famous virtuous ladies like Lucretia, he gives vent to furious attacks on all the wicked women of classical lore.

Jerome was also responsible for giving wide publicity to the saying of Sextus the Pythagorean, 'He who loves his wife too ardently is an adulterer.' This was much quoted later.

It is likely that much anti-feminist writing in the Middle Ages owes its origin to Jerome's example, both in formalised attacks and also in the arbitrary dragging-in of a classical tag to add bite to an argument. If Jerome, in expounding Micah 7, verses 5–7, felt it appropriate to quote the famous saying of Virgil from *Aeneid* IV '*varium et mutabile semper femina*' [woman is always a fickle and changeable creature], it is not surprising that Walter of Coincy, a monk who wrote a book of instruction for nuns, should have quoted from Ovid's *Amores* '*casta est quam nemo rogavit*' to show that women were chaste only if they had no opportunity to behave otherwise.

When one is tracing Jerome's influence on medieval attitudes one is somewhat hampered by the fact that he is often quoted without attribution. Plagiarism was not the crime then that it is now. So we can find passages taken over verbatim from Jerome without a mention of his name anywhere.

But there are plenty of acknowledged quotations, and these are found both in clerical and secular literature. It is not possible in the scope of this chapter to make more than a brief mention of examples.

Abélard quotes Jerome to encourage his readers to a life of austerity. But it is interesting to notice that both Abélard and Héloïse use Jerome's arguments for their own purposes. (This is something they may have learned from Jerome.) Héloïse, for example, uses Jerome's arguments against marriage to justify her proposal to remain Abélard's concubine and not destroy his career by marrying him. But surely if she was really following the spirit of Jerome's teaching she would renounce totally her sexual involvement with Abélard and re-embrace chastity with fervour! Perhaps Jerome's device of calling on support from pagan literature encouraged Héloïse to point to some of Jerome's sources as advisers of free love – a use of his material which would of course have horrified Jerome. Abélard uses Jerome's imagery from the Song of Songs to encourage Héloïse in the monastic life, emphasising that she is now the Bride of Christ.

A more detailed study of the influence of Jerome's attitudes to women on medieval literature would have to take account of such works as *Holy Maidenhood*, Walter Map's *De Nugis Curialium*, the *Romance of the Rose*, and *Lamentations of Matheolus*, among others. Most important however would be the works of Chaucer.

Chaucer quotes from Jerome in several of his works, most notably in the Prologue to *The Wife of Bath's Tale*. It is in this Prologue, with its references to, and its quotations from, the *Against Jovinian*, that we see most clearly how wide Jerome's influence was. I do not think that Chaucer would have used the *Against Jovinian* in just this way had it not been a well-known piece of writing in his day. He both refers to it by name as if it would be known to his readers, and then uses it subtly and artfully for an audience in the know to enjoy.

The Wife of Bath's Prologue is larded with quotations from the *Against Jovinian*. Chaucer, that master of irony, puts the words of one of the greatest anti-feminists of all time into the mouth of a woman who unashamedly advocates sexual enjoyment and licence.

Jerome's work is a carefully constructed piece of polemic. It is composed of quotations from Jovinian, and Jerome's heated response to these, quotations from the Bible in general and the Apostle Paul in particular, anecdotes from classical literature, and the long anti-feminist tirade of Theophrastus.

When one looks at *The Wife of Bath*'s Prologue it shows some of these features of construction also, and just as Jerome uses the rhetorical device of question and answer, statement and refutation, so does the Wife. When she quotes or paraphrases Jerome she picks and chooses passages which suit her purpose, adroitly omitting whatever does not appeal to her, or wilfully misunderstanding so that she can appear to be claiming Jerome's support for her own viewpoint.

One or two brief examples of the Wife's reflections will have to suffice. That much-married lady mentions that she has heard that because Jesus went only once to a wedding she should marry only once. She objects that she has never heard on good authority just how many husbands one may have; is bigamy possible, or octogamy? This highly unusual word comes from Jerome who declares that once one has gone beyond a single marriage – his only approved number (and that of course with reservations) – it matters little whether you have two, three, four or even eight marriages.

The Wife says that since, as far as she can discover, God has forbidden neither marriage not subsequent marriages she shall continue happily in her present ways. After all, where would virginity spring from if not from marriage? This is exactly the purpose of marriage as stated by Jerome.

One can understand and appreciate the cleverness of Chaucer's portrait of the wife of Bath only if one is familiar with Jerome's *Anti-Jovinian*, but one must not attach too much blame to Jerome here. He could not have foreseen the use to which his writings would be put.

Finally, while we have to acknowledge sadly that Jerome's

strident criticisms of women damaged their position seriously for centuries to come, we must recognise that he was zealous for the truth as he saw it, and his view of the truth was that which was prevalent in his time.

NOTES

1. See my articles on 'The Vulgate Genesis and Jerome's Attitudes to Women' in *Studia Patristica* Vol. XVIII (Pergamon Press, Oxford and New York, 1982), and in OTWSA No. 20/21 (Pretoria, 1982), pp. 1–20.

7

Saints and Sybils:
Hildegard of Bingen to Teresa of Avila

Benedicta Ward

How could I presume to teach or advise you who are favoured with hidden knowledge and in whom the influence of Christ's anointing still lives so that you have no need of teaching, for you are said to be able to search the secrets of heaven and to discern by the light of the Holy Spirit things that are beyond the knowledge of man. It is rather for me to beg that you may not forget me before God or those who are united to me in spiritual fellowship.[1]

That is a remarkably humble letter from the greatest theologian of the twelfth century, Bernard of Clairvaux. It is his reply to a letter he had received from the Abbess of Mount St Rupert, Hildegard, who describes herself as '*paupercula femina forma*' ['a poor little womanly figure']. Bernard, the theologian of prayer, is filled with admiration for one who prays but does not analyse; there are two spheres, separate and distinct, and it is the woman who prays who is admired by the man who analyses and not vice versa. Four hundred years later in the relationship between John of the Cross and Teresa of Avila there has been a change in which both mystics also apply their minds to the analysis of experience. The change is in the women visionaries rather than in the men theologians and it seems worth comparing Hildegard of Bingen and Teresa of Avila in some detail in order to see where the differences lie. Much of the contrast they present may be attributed to differences of literary genre, of culture or simply of temperament but it may be of deeper significance to explore the exalted position of women in the medieval Church as true 'theologians', that is, as seers and sybils, visionaries and intercessors, and to see why they were so respected and if this position was changed then they turned their minds also to the analysis of the life of prayer. With Hildegard and Teresa who wrote so much and in such variety it is only possible to indicate here where some of the differences lie and to offer a tentative suggestion about the reasons behind them.

Bernard of Clairvaux wrote about the journey of the soul to God with such insight that he influenced deeply and permanently the way in which prayer was both experienced and discussed in his own day as well as later. It is at first sight remarkable that he should have been so impressed by the prophetic and mystical experiences of a woman, but he makes it clear that Hildegard was everything he admired and, he thought, failed himself to become. Above all she was taught by God, the clear structures of learning which Bernard deplored had never closed her mind to divine truth; she saw by what she called the divine light and she saw truly. Like the unlettered lay brothers at Clairvaux, she heard and saw the world of the spirit directly. The parallel Bernard saw between them was in part, of course, a fantasy; Hildegard constantly claims to be 'simple' and 'unlearned' but this modest phrase is deceptive. Unlike the lay brothers of the Cistercian Order, many of whom really were unable to read and write, Hildegard knew Latin and dictated books of considerable complexity. She was a woman of renown in her times, and her writings comprise almost the greatest range of literature of any medieval author. What Bernard meant and what Hildegard claimed, was, rather, a lack of formal academic training. What they agreed upon in a positive sense was that just because of this 'ignorance' she could receive direct inspiration from God which could not be argued with. Moreover, it was an authority that even the most rational minds of the twelfth century accepted as final: what Hildegard wanted done, was done, not on account of her undoubted ability either as a writer or as a monastic superior, but because she was held to enjoy a knowledge far superior to any merely rational method of inquiry.

Hildegard was admired by many besides Bernard. He recommended her to Eugenius, the Cistercian Pope, and arranged for him to meet Hildegard at Trier on his way to Rheims for the trial of Gilbert de la Porée since Bingen is on the Rhine only thirty miles from Trier. Eugenius became one of Hildegard's fervent admirers and they wrote letters to one another; she corresponded with successive popes, Anastasius IV, Adrian IV and Alexander III; she wrote to churchmen, to religious, and also to secular rulers such as Conrad III and his son Frederick Barbarossa, Henry II of England and his wife Eleanor of Aquitaine, the Empress Irene and Philip, Count of Flanders. She undertook journeys, preached to monks in their monasteries and clergy in their synods, and laymen in towns; she gave spiritual counsel, she exorcised, she argued and she prophesied. She was clearly a woman of very great force of character, but all she did was in the name of the light which was not her own, a claim that was recognised and accepted.

Hildegard was respected not in spite of her tendency to strange and emotional ecstasies but because of them: they marked her out as a prophetess. It seems that she was not suddenly visited by heavenly inspiration as a nun and abbess but had been accustomed to such visions from early childhood. In 1141 when she was forty-two she felt herself commissioned to reveal the visions, which she did by dictating them to two close friends, the monk Volmar and the nun Richarda:

> A fiery light of the greatest brilliancy coming from the opened heavens poured into all my brain and kindled in my heart and breast, a flame that warms but does not consume as the sun heats everything over which he casts his rays . . . I said and wrote . . . not according to the curious invention of my heart but as I saw, heard and perceived them in a heavenly way through the secret mysteries of God. And again I heard a voice from heaven saying unto me, 'Cry aloud therefore and write thus.'[2]

This description, couched in the personal and emotional language of the twelfth century, is nevertheless replete with traditional imagery. The 'prayer of fire' associated with the descent of the Holy Spirit is a main theme of Eastern theology and the final quotation links her ecstasy with the Book of Revelation and the vision of St John (cf. Rev. 1.19). Moreover, her revelations belong to the tradition of compunction, that piercing of the heart by fear and love for a further inner knowledge of the divine which Gregory the Great articulated for the West and which formed the basis of such popular meditations as those of Anselm of Canterbury.[3] At times it is the theme of wonder and glory that seizes her:

> I saw as it were the mystery of God in the southern sky, a wonderful and beautiful image in the form of a man whose face was so beautiful and brilliant that I could more easily have looked into the sun . . . 'I am the high and the fiery power that kindled all living sparks . . . I burn in the fiery life of the substance of divinity above the beauty of the fields, and I shine in the waters and I burn in the stars . . .'[4]

At other times, it is the terror of distance from God and the burden of sinful mortality that oppresses her:

> Whither am I, a pilgrim, going? Into the valley of death. In what way do I go? The way of error. What consolation do I have? That of a pilgrim. Others deride me, saying, 'Where is your honour now?' Oh, where am I? Whence did I come? What consolation do I seek in this captivity? How can I break my chains? What eye can see my wounds? What hands will anoint them with oil? Who will show pity on my grief? Therefore He will hear my cry.[5]

Such deeply emotional and self-revealing experiences by no means removed Hildegard into a realm of mysterious ineptitude. What she wrote about was not only or even especially religious. She was interested in botany, in medicine, in minerals, she composed music and her visions inspired pictures of a wild and impressive kind. Her advice was very practical, and her administration of her abbey so effective that the small and rather undistinguished little group which she met at Disiboden (when she arrived there as a child of eight to be educated by the hermitess Jutta) had, when she died as abbess in 1179 at the age of eighty-two, become a large and flourishing abbey on excellent land at Bingen. This move was an example of the force of a visionary woman upon very practical men. The monks closest to her convent as confessors viewed her proposal to move from Disiboden with alarm and hostility. They were unwilling to lose both nuns, who were without exception and by a deliberate policy of the abbess, high-born ladies, and their endowments. Hildegard wrote to the monks in these terms when she heard of their opposition to the move:

> In accordance with what I had seen in my true vision I said to the father abbot, 'The serene light says, you shall be father to our provost (the monk Volmar) and father of the salvation of the souls of the daughters of my mystic garden. But their alms do not belong to you or to your brothers – your cloister should be a refuge for these women and if you are determined to go on with your perverse proposals, raging against us, you will be like the Amalekites . . . justice will destroy you. And when I, poor little creature, had with these words petitioned the abbot and his confrères for the freehold of the site and domains of my daughters they all granted it to me, entering the transfer in a codex.[6]

Hildegard was listened to and respected as a sybil, as a prophet, one through whom the Spirit of God spoke most clearly but at the same time her influence and practical activity were undoubted. In this she was a highly significant figure for her times. There is no doubt that the twelfth century saw a change in the kind of activities open to women. The political and economic power they wielded with ease and confidence earlier was drastically limited. They were excluded from Latin education by the rise of the universities as never before. The disaster of the cult of courtly love isolated them by glorifying them. But in certain spheres the women prospered. One was the emergence of vernacular literature and another was the prophetic and mystical role which opened increasingly to them.

From Hildegard of Bingen in the twelfth century to Teresa of Avila in the sixteenth there was an increasing number of prophetesses, many of them women of discernment and influence. The thirteenth and fourteenth centuries in particular saw an explosion of women visionaries: the great ladies of Helfta, Gertrude and Mechtild, and particularly their younger contemporary Mechtild of Hackborn; Elizabeth of Schonau; Hadewijch, Beatrice of Nazareth, Margeret of Oignt, Catherine of Sienna, Catherine of Genoa, Bridget of Sweden, Margery Kempe, Julian of Norwich, to name only the most obvious. Like Hildegard, these were women visionaries, highly respected and attended to: dreams, visions, prophecies, trances, locutions, suspension of the faculties, all were there. With the more able and controlled visionaries, they committed their revelations to writings which exercised influence and commanded respect. Of course, men were also equally open to the influence of mystical experience but it seems that this mostly took the form of analysis of the life of prayer in writing, exhortation to it in preaching, or counsel about it. Many of the revelations of the women mystics were written about by men by whom they were highly, even hysterically respected, as having a specially direct and mysterious contact with divinity which was its own justification. Though deeply immersed in the central activity of prayer with all its demands for solitude, silence and detachment, the women visionaries were also active, busy women, aware of the world and its needs, and prepared to involve themselves and their experiences of prayer in the affairs of their day. Catherine of Sienna, for instance, was at the centre of ecclesiastical politics for most of her adult life yet was pre-eminently renowned for her visions and ecstatic experiences. One can only conclude that unlike ourselves, the Middle Ages regarded the exterior phenomena of the mystic as a passport to credibility, not the reverse. This link between paranormal phenomena, sound theology and practical common sense presents certain problems for those in a very different psychological and theological atmosphere. There are perhaps at least two preliminary differences in the understanding of reality to bear in mind when approaching this question, which were true for the sixteenth as well as the twelfth century.

    The first major difference to notice is the extent to which medieval theology was linked to ancient concepts of anthropology. The human biology of the ancient world depended on the theory of the elements and the humours. Man was the microcosm of the universe, and both were made up of the elements of earth, air, fire and water. Man and woman together formed the perfect human being and the elements were divided between them: men were predominantly air and fire, women earth and water. Air and fire made for the critical intellect, earth signified fruitfulness and water was a spiritual principal which opened women to visions and dreams. The twelfth century pushed many things to logical conclusions, it was a great age for categorising and making lists and they did it with this world view also. Man issued from the hand of God, male/female. The airy and fiery elements opened him to reason, the earthy, watery elements to divinity unalloyed. Hildegard put it like this:

'Oh humans, look at the human being! for it contains heaven and earth and all other creatures within itself and is one form and all other creatures hide in it.'[7]

The part of this whole which was directly open to heaven was, therefore, feminine; woman was man's love, his heart, and his direct route to the powers of the air. She was therefore seen as being by her very nature the dreamer, the prophet, the visionary.

Secondly, there was a different understanding throughout the Middle Ages of the significance of the flesh. On the one hand, extreme illness was not regarded as merely unfortunate; it could be a gift, opening the mind to heaven: Hildegard, Teresa and many, perhaps all, other women mystics began their inner, mystical life through this liberating breaking of the external senses in severe illnesses. On the other hand, interior vision was naturally accompanied by external phenomena: the visionaries saw, heard, smelled, touched, even tasted the celestial visions, reacting visibly to inner experience with their senses. These physical phenomena were recorded vividly and with reverence, a fact which is often forgotten by those who concentrate on the very strong and theologically sensible content of the visions. For the Middle Ages, the reactions of the body were not seen as improper but as authenticating. Where people were peculiarly open to God it was expected that the effect would show in their bodies. This is not perhaps completely alien to our experience. After all, human beings only have five senses to register whatever happens to them; the spirit does not invent new and spiritual matter for itself. Even now, it is a common experience that serious illness can become the gateway to deeper apprehensions of reality. On the other hand, great personal grief or complete desolation does not make one pale and romantic but is so disorientating that it will be as likely as not to cause vomiting and a blinding headache. So the coming of the Spirit of God on a human being was thought to use the normal make-up of that person. Thus, the eyes closed, the breathing changed, those so visited seemed to speak automatically, to rise from the ground, become rigid and immovable or even impassible for hours on end; they heard sounds inaudible and saw sights invisible to others – all these things earlier ages took for granted and even required in their mystics.

Such physical reactions might alert people to the presence of something unusual but in spite of this it would still seem to us that such personal revelation was in itself uncheckable. If I say I have a vision, you cannot say I have not. The problem of authentication of visionaries has always exercised serious-minded people, but in earlier ages the external symptoms had greater weight. There were women visionaries whose ecstasies seem to us pointless, neither significant nor helpful to others. Perhaps Christina the Astonishing falls into this category as someone we regard as simply neurotic. She is said to have been frequently in trances so deep that they were mistaken for death; on one occasion her body had been carried into church for burial when she revived. At once, her corpse flew up to the roof where she perched like a bird until the people were cleared out, for it was known that Christina could not stand the smell of human flesh. Among her more pointless escapades was her habit of getting into ovens where she sat down, presumably under the impression that she was a bun. She would climb on to the mill wheel and go round with it, and once she sat down in the font when it was full of water.[8] This tomboy athletic style of sainthood seems to us unedifying since totally devoid of theological or moral content but her contemporaries were prepared to accept what they did not understand; there was sufficient respect for her trances for her to be included in the calendar of the saints. The reactions of the body were regarded as the work of the Spirit upon flesh and that was sufficient for wonder and awe; they were signs of the hidden approval of God, beyond human judgments and opinions.

While these two ideas about the human person and about the significance of the flesh are unfamiliar to the twentieth century, they continued long past the sixteenth century to shape European notions of reality. It is not, therefore, that a change occurred in the sixteenth century. Rather, a new caution began to be felt about the significance of bodily phenomena in prayer. There was a new stress on what was intellectually orthodox, accompanied by more caution about the possibility of demonic deception especially for the untutored mind. In a united Europe, where Christian teaching was mostly clearly articulated and heretics were few, visionaries had been easily accepted and indeed cherished, their orthodoxy unquestioned. In the sixteenth century under the pressure of heresy, the evidence of the experiences of the ecstatic visionaries was received with a new caution. Those faced with a visionary who might well be a heretic and perhaps, like Elizabeth Barton, the Fair Maid of Kent, used in secular political matters, could no longer be impressed solely by her states of trance; they might suspect quite other spirits of speaking through her. A vision itself was no longer authenticating. Visionaries had to be examined for uprightness of life and their visions had to be checked by their content; was what they said in ecstasy worth saying? Was it in accordance with Scripture? With church doctrine as agreed by the consensus of Christian people? Did it lead to the virtues of charity, faith, hope, peace? Was it edifying to others?

Such analysis did increasingly take place and one of the foremost in offering such criteria for authenticity was a woman who was herself subject to extreme and alarming mystical states. Teresa of Avila was within this tradition of women visionaries. Like them, she was a woman of great influence and continual activity; like her predecessors, she claimed ignorance of both Latin and scholastic methods, the traditional *deprecatio* which nevertheless was intended to show that the writer's mind was not confined along particular and defined ways. She writes, she says, about what she understands from within, not from exterior information. Like most of the women mystics after Hildegard, Teresa wrote in the vernacular. Subject to trances, visions, ecstasies, she, like the rest, was widely consulted and was most highly regarded for her prayer; so highly regarded that people would act upon what she said. But there was a change; for one thing, the Inquisition was demanding examination of those who experienced paranormal states; and for another, Teresa herself offered detailed analysis of such experiences as part of a whole structure of the life of prayer.

In the last books of the *Life* and in the *Interior Castle*, Teresa set down a great deal about the different kinds of visions experienced by those who pray.[9] They were, perhaps, merely sensory, perhaps imaginary, perhaps intellectual; if accompanied by physical phenomena, that was a sign of a weak integration of body and spirit and should be disregarded. And always the central check for the one praying was perseverance in the way of charity which is the following of Christ. Teresa did not refuse to give attention to the subject of visions and saw them as a valid part of the life of prayer, but it is clear that her approach was more subtle than that of Hildegard.

Teresa herself was seized by ecstasy of one kind or another for most of her life, and in order to communicate anything about these moments of vision, she used new images rather than old arguments or descriptions. Like all the mystics, she used language of a poetic, mysterious nature, but here joined to an analytic intellect, which combined both the experiential and the expository sides of mystical writing in a new way. Her use of images in describing the way of prayer is very like the explicitly visionary language of Hildegard. For instance, the central image of the *Interior Castle* is a crystal ball shaped like a castle; it is described with intense imaginative beauty, matching anything in the visions of Hildegard or Mechtild, and it was revealed to her first of all, it seems, in a vision:

> On the eve of the festival of the Most Holy Trinity, she (Teresa) was thinking what subject she should choose for this treatise, when God who disposes all things in due form and order granted this desire of hers and gave her a subject. He showed her a most beautiful crystal globe, made in the shape of a castle, and containing seven mansions, in the seventh and innermost of which was the King of Glory, illuminating and beautifying them all.[10]

It sounds very like a vision of Hildegard, but there is a distinct difference. Teresa did not simply experience a vision, but saw the way in which she was to analyse prayer in the form of a vision. Like the men who wrote about prayer, she provided an interpretation. Given this vision, she asked herself questions about its precise significance for others. She saw the crystal ball as the soul, the castle is within, and every visionary detail was clearly interpreted according to her understanding of prayer. The image in the vision was linked to the Scriptures and she had good precedent for seeing the 'many mansions' of the Father's house (John 14.2) as the person, the temple of God which is within. Other writers had used the image, though not in quite the same way; the *Proslogion* of Anselm, for instance, begins with an invitation into the 'inner chamber' where one seeks God who is within, the ground of being, while Hugh of St Victor used a particular house, Noah's ark, for his discussion of the life of the soul in prayer.[11] The difference is that Teresa presented the image as a result of a direct vision from God, and with this she combined a strict analysis of the life of prayer. The interior castle was not with Teresa simply an amazing celestial building whose every piece might be replete with changing, shifting images of wonder; it provided, rather, a structure for articulating rational thoughts about prayer.

For Teresa such images were not an end in themselves. She considered prayer, and particularly any visionary experience, to be linked indissolubly with asceticism; not as a way into prayer but a result of it. From the other end, so to speak, the body had its place in prayer also for Teresa, not as the vehicle of divinity so much as the place where love planted in the heart would then overflow into all the senses and all of life. In this sense it is interesting to note that for herself, 'betrothal to the Lord' meant acute desolation and the inner rooms of the crystal castle were full of darkness.

It is necessary to distinguish between Teresa's deliberate and conscious use of imagery and her accounts of experiences of a paranormal nature, but in a way they come from the same apprehension of life. Through both she says prayer is not either emotional or intellectual; mind and emotion are linked to the flesh for her as much as for Hildegard, and she was well aware that the impact of the divine upon the human body could take extraordinary forms. There are what Teresa calls 'lesions', that is, gaps between vision and experience. For example, absorption in prayer can so dislocate the normal unity of the self that the one who prays may begin to drop things, forget things, not react on a natural level very quickly, become clumsy, not quite functioning, something that was reverenced in earlier mystics but with Teresa is treated with a brisk compassion. Though Teresa never denied her own experiences of trance and vision, such manifestations were to be hidden and disregarded. She saw them as 'the least of the gifts' – not things to be afraid of, but not to be regarded or sought. They might be of God or they might not; if they were, then there would be an increase of charity in daily life: charity towards men, love towards God, a humility which thinks itself unworthy of notice. For herself, she used to test such revelations by asking others whose opinion she respected about them. There had been enough false mystics and some of them close at hand for her to have learned not to trust the externals even for herself with the simplicity of the earlier mystics.

No doubt Teresa would have classed most of Hildegard's visions as 'corporal', a kind of vision with which Teresa says she was not personally acquainted. Her own visions she called either 'imaginary' or 'intellectual', and she discussed them for their content and meaning alone. What was external in visionary states was for her at best peripheral, at worst a temptation to pride; they were to be examined with care and related to the whole of Christian life. The most famous of her own experiences, when she felt that her heart was being pierced by the fiery spear of a seraph, is an example both of the similarity of language about mystical experience and the difference between its apprehension in the early Middle Ages and the sixteenth century.[12] Hildegard described a vision of seraphs in terms remarkably similar to those of Teresa:

> These signify the Seraphim because they are burning with the love of God, having a very great desire for the vision of Him . . . the secrets of God appear in them wonderfully as they do also in those loving souls who seek eternal life in the sincerity of a pure heart. These love God ardently and embrace him with a pure desire.[13]

In her *Life* Teresa also speaks of a seraph and of love, and this is one of the very rare passages where she describes a 'corporal' vision of her own:

> It pleased the Lord that I should sometimes see the following vision. I would see beside me, on my left hand, an angel in bodily form – a type of vision which I am not in the habit of seeing

except very rarely . . . He was not tall but short, and very beautiful, his face so aflame that he appeared to be one of the highest types of angels who seem to be all afire . . . In his hand I saw a long golden spear and at the end of the iron tip I seemed to see a point of fire. With this he seemed to pierce my heart . . . he left me completely afire with a great love for God. The pain was so sharp that it made me utter several moans . . .[14]

It is clear that Hildegard and Teresa write within the same tradition of angelic visions but there are significant differences. Both connect the seraphim with light and with the inner mysteries of the vision of God and with desire for him. The metaphor of fire has been used for centuries about prayer connected both with the heart, the most central part of the person and with the Holy Spirit. While Hildegard records what she 'sees' with amazement and delight and regards her vision as something to be communicated to all, Teresa writes about the 'fire' as a personal and inner experience of immense pain, and of something so intimate that she was distressed when others connected such things with her. It is significant that the transverberation happened at the end of her quiet life as a simple Carmelite nun; it overflowed into the next years of active service of others until her death. The famous statue by Bernini of Teresa with her heart being pierced by a seraph says nothing else – love in the centre of the soul, so that it affects every action and thought. To refer that baroque expression of devotion to Teresa is perhaps hardly to our taste or in line with our view of her; nor is the equally well-known poem upon the book and the picture of the 'Seraphical Teresa':

> O thou undaunted daughter of desires
> by all thy dower of lights and fires
> by all the eagle in thee, all the dove
> by all thy lives and deaths of love
> by thy large draughts of intellectual day
> and by thy thirsts of love more large than they
> by all thy brim-filled bowls of fierce desire
> by thy last morning draught of liquid fire
> by the full kingdom of that final kiss

that seized thy parting soul and sealed thee His
by all the heaven thou hadst in Him
fair sister of the seraphim
by all of him we have in thee
leave nothing of myself in me;
let me so read thy life that I
unto all life of mine may die.[15]

It sounds much more like Hildegard than Teresa, and the reality
which completed that 'final kiss' did not seem to Teresa like
anything of the kind. A few days before her death, Teresa was
carried reluctantly in extreme sickness to the house of a friend
who wanted her there while she, Donna Anna, bore a child, a
sentimental desire to treat Teresa as a saint which she disliked
and mocked. There on 9th October, 1571, she died; she was
repeating over and over again Psalm 51: 'the sacrifice of God is
a troubled spirit, a broken and a contrite heart, O God, thou wilt
not despise.'

The writings of or about the medieval mystics reveal some shifts
in the way revelation was understood and received from the twelfth
century to the sixteenth. With Hildegard, the fact of her ecstatic
states was authenticating for her other activities; their place in
the whole tradition of Christian life was taken for granted; both
she and others were simply impressed by the actual experiences
themselves which were seen as authentication given by God himself.
The visionary states themselves created awe and were left open
for interpretation; the activity and actual influence of the visionaries
were simply the results of the impact of mysterious divinity and
it was rare to find any of the early visionaries exploring and
analysing their visions as a scheme of prayer or of life in detail.
Teresa was as much a visionary as any of them, and exceeded
even Hildegard in the activities of her work for the Carmelite
Reform and in the force of her influence on others. But there is
a most significant difference between them, for where Hildegard
merely saw, Teresa analysed and classified. She applied her mind
to the analysis of any visionary experiences, her own or others,
and made them a part of a whole structure for understanding and
pursuing the life of prayer and charity. In the case of all the visionary

women, there is a unifying theme of direct and intimate receptivity in prayer towards divinity which was seen as their 'theology', even when it was eventually combined with the analytic presentation of prayer. At least with Teresa, the analysis of visions did not diminish their value as a direct participation in divine life, however this may have been later. With her, the rational intellect was seen as balancing and not negating – though at times as subsidiary to – intuitive understanding, a balance which seems to have swung in the opposite direction for far too long a period.

NOTES

1. *Letters of St Bernard of Clairvaux*, trans. Bruno Scott James (London, 1953), Letter 390, p. 460.

2. *Hildegardis Scivias*, ed. A. Fuhrkotter, A. Carlevaris, *Corpus Christianorum Continuatio Mediaevalis*, xlii–xliii A (Turnhout, 1978), Preface, pp. 3–4 (hereinafter referred to as *Scivias*). Hildegard's other works are found in PL 197. Of the recent English versions of Hildegard's works, I have either used the translations provided in Peter Dronke's excellent chapter, 'Hildegard of Bingen' in *Women Writers in the Middle Ages* (Cambridge, 1984) (hereinafter referred to as Dronke) or attempted my own translation of Hildegard's unusual Latin.

3. Cf. *Prayers and Meditations of St Anselm of Canterbury with the Proslogion*, trans. with introduction, Benedicta Ward (Penguin Books, 1979/87).

4. Hildegard, *Liber Divinorum Operum Simplicis Hominis*, Vision 1, PL 197, col. 74.

5. Hildegard, *Scivias*, 4th Vision, p. 62.

6. Hildegard, *Letters*, PL 197, col. 1065 (Dronke, p. 153).

7. Hildegard, *Causae et Curae*, Dronke p. 172; Latin Text, Dronke p. 241.

8. Thomas de Cantimpre, *Vita Baetae Christinae Mirabilis Trundonopoli in Hasbania*, Acta Sanctorum Jul.1,5 (Paris, 1868) pp. 637–60; English translation by M. King in *Medieval Women's Visionary Literature*, ed. E.A. Petroff (Oxford, 1986) pp. 184–9.

9. (The Works of St Teresa will be referred to in the translations of E. Allison Peers (London, 1946) by their English titles with references to chapters only.) Teresa, *The Interior Castle*, VI.ix,4ff. Cf. *Revelation* IV,14. Teresa's discussion of visions is analysed and compared with the teaching of St John of the Cross by E.W. Trueman Dicken,

The Crucible of Love: a Study in the Mysticism of St Teresa and St John of the Cross (London, 1936), pp. 374–406.

10.   Teresa, *Interior Castle*, Introduction, p. 10.

11.   Hugh of St Victor, *De Arce Noe Morali*, PL 176.

12.   Teresa, *Interior Castle*, cap. v; *Life*, xviii. Teresa's teaching on union is discussed by E. Truman Dicken (op. cit. note 9), pp. 407–30.

13.   Hildegard, *Scivias*, vi, pp. 106–7.

14.   Teresa, *Life*, xxix.

15.   Richard Crashaw, 'The Flaming Heart: Upon the Book and Picture of the Seraphical Teresa'.

8

Richard Hooker and the
Ordination of Women to the Priesthood

Stephen Sykes

A more dutifull and religious way for us were to admire the
wisedome of God, which shineth in the bewtifull varietie of all
things, but most in the manifold and yet harmonious dissimilitude
of those wayes, whereby his Church upon earth is guided from
age to age, throughout all generations of men.[1]

I

When Anglicans confront the fact that the Roman Catholic Church
deems the ordination of women to the priesthood not to be in
accordance with God's plan for his Church,[2] they are obliged to
reflect on their own understanding of the Church. There are many
Anglicans, perhaps a majority, for whom the firm opposition of the
Pope and the Sacred Congregation for the Doctrine of the Faith
is a most serious obstacle. Among these will undoubtedly be some
who hold more or less secretly that the churches of the Anglican
communion have no basis of authority independent of the Papacy,
and for whom, therefore, a Papal veto is simply final. Their identity
as Anglicans will, of course, be severely tried by a decision to ordain
women to the priesthood. But since they make no intellectual case
for their present allegiance, they can hardly complain of any
inconsistency in such an Anglican development. A much larger and
more serious number of Anglicans, however, hold strongly the
argument from tradition, in which Roman Catholics and Eastern
Orthodox agree, and will feel on ecumenical grounds the

inadvisability of any movement which increases the gulf between Anglicans and the non-Protestant world.

I have on a number of occasions attempted to point out how misleading is the mental map which simply spreads the denominations out in a straight line, and places Anglicanism midway between Rome and wherever it is thought the headquarters of undifferentiated Protestantism may lie.[3] There have been at least three versions of *via media* Anglicanism. In the sixteenth century, Anglicans, together with Lutherans, saw themselves as midway between Rome and Anabaptism. By the mid-seventeenth century the Church of England was developing an apologetic self-understanding over against independency and presbyterianism, as representative of left-wing Protestantism, which in the Tractarian recension became *the via media* between Rome and 'popular Protestantism', as defined by John Henry Newman. The history of these variations demonstrates the instability and inadequacy of the model, which is, in any case, on any rational reflection unacceptably crude. It has, moreover, inhibited Anglicans from the necessary attempt to articulate their own understanding of the Church. Knowing that some Anglicans are 'virtually' Protestants and others 'virtually' Romans, the straight line model has suggested that Anglicanism can be 'comprehensive' by the simple expedient of adopting the ecclesiologies of others. But this is an illusion, the poverty of which is rapidly disclosed by ecumenical contact. For, one discovers, the Orthodox, Roman Catholics and Lutherans all claim 'comprehensiveness' – and accuse Anglicans of incoherence. Anglicans have to learn that a comprehensive church needs to articulate a doctrine of the Church precisely in order to justify its very comprehensiveness.[4]

One needs, therefore, an Anglican doctrine of the Church in order to understand what it is that Anglicans are doing in ordaining, or proposing to ordain women to the Church's priesthood. An 'Anglican doctrine of the Church' is not the same thing as a doctrine of the Anglican Church. The latter would be, however useful in practice, inadequate for the task of interpreting what it is that is done when people are ordained to the 'ministry of Christ's Holy, Catholic and Apostolic Church'.

What is required is a Christian doctrine of the Church, making claims to evangelical and catholic truth, which Anglicans, who are as a matter of fact a distinct denomination in Christendom, can accept as true. Whether such a doctrine strikes other people as 'distinctively Anglican' is for them to judge. What is needed is an understanding of the Church corresponding to the norms of catholic doctrine as Anglicans believe them to be, and which makes sense of their witness, experience and hope.

II

One part of such a reflection should entail the examination of the acknowledged classics of Anglican theology of the past. The acute failure of theological nerve precipitated by the violent internal polemics of the nineteenth century assuredly did not afflict Anglicans of earlier centuries. Among the theological justifications of the stance of the Church of England offered then, Richard Hooker's apologia for the Elizabethan settlement, *Of the Laws of Ecclesiastical Polity*, is pre-eminent. Moreover Hooker is precisely that kind of theologian against whose understanding of the Church Anglicans should test these modern proposals, since his encounter with what has recently been named 'moderate puritanism'[5] made him sensitive to those particular issues relating to tradition which cause modern Anglicans such anxiety when confronted by the innovatory ordination of women to the priesthood.

The thesis of this paper is that it is entirely consistent with the theological method of the most famous Anglican writer perhaps of the whole of Anglican history, Richard Hooker, that women should be ordained to the priesthood. It is an argument whose intention is to take seriously the objection that such ordinations constitute a break of the invariable tradition of the Church from the days of the apostles. I have two further objectives in mind. The first is to exhibit the thought of a major Christian theologian wrestling with the problem of church order in such a way as to show how it can and should be related to particular times and places. And the second is to demonstrate that it is possible to hold both that a particular church order is divinely ordained and also that it is not immutable. The severing of this particular connection is of especial importance, for those who like myself cannot draw from the conclusion that the

Church must today ordain women to the priesthood the inference that it was in error not to do so in earlier centuries. The genesis of this paper lay in a question and a hunch. Based on the realisation that Richard Hooker and William Shakespeare were contemporaries, the question arose whether the theologian showed any signs of interest in the debate about women which so fascinated Tudor and Elizabethan society.[6] On the speedy discovery that virtually all of Hooker's references to women were of a sturdily conservative kind, as we shall see, the hypothesis presented itself that, despite this standard sixteenth century patriarchalism, the position espoused by Hooker on the broader issue of order in the Church might lend itself to serious treatment of the grounds for the ordination of women. What follows is the result of the pursuit of this hunch. Begun perhaps in a somewhat lighthearted desire to enlist the support of one of the supposed 'fathers' of Anglo-Catholicism, it has resulted in an increased respect for the profundity and subtlety of Hooker's theological stance, and especially for his readiness to take seriously the social reality of the Christian Church in time and history; so that I have found my growing conviction of the importance of the study of social history for the Christian Church at every stage of its life to be met and deepened by Hooker's insistence on the dual character of the Church, 'being both a societie and a societie supernaturall'.[7]

III

There are three pages in the *Laws* in which Hooker makes passing but explicit references to the status of women. The first is in the Preface, where Hooker acknowledges the fact that women were prominent as recruits to the puritan cause, but takes this to be an indication of the inferiority of the rational grounds for puritanism, on the assumption that the judgments of women are 'commonlie weakest by the reason of their sex'.[8] Hooker admits the 'eagernesse of their affection' and their 'naturall inclination into pittie', but observes with some disdain the opportunities women enjoy 'to procure encouragements for their brethren' and the delight they take 'in giving verie large and particular intelligence, how all neere about them stand affected as concerning the same cause'.[9] They are, in a word, gossips.

In the second passage, the point at issue is the emergency baptism of infants by women, especially by midwives. The immediate background to this was the objection of the Admonitioners that the Prayer Book had not specifically forbidden such baptisms, as had Calvin and Bullinger, on the grounds that it was a superstitious use of the sacrament.[10] Hooker's view followed Luther, Tyndale and the general Catholic tradition in accepting the legality and validity of baptism by women, as part of his defence of the view that baptism is 'generally [i.e. universally] necessary to salvation'. Lay baptism in cases of urgent necessity is consistent with this stance, and Hooker strenuously resists the apparent corollary that women can be 'ministers in the Church of God' which, he tartly remarks, would be a 'grosse absurditie' in the light of the Apostle Paul's injunctions not to let women teach (quoting 1 Tim. 2.12 and 1 Cor. 14.34). Here Hooker refers to the (fourth century) document entitled the *Apostolic Constitutions*, which he held, together with the majority of his contemporaries, to have been written by Clement of Rome in the first century. In this document we find a specific injunction that a woman may not baptise, which Hooker is at some pains to gloss as a prohibition designed to deter the rash and presumptuous from turning what is lawful in necessity into something more common.[11]

The last example of a reference to women occurs in the section on matrimony in Book V, where Hooker is attempting to meet Puritan objections to the ceremonies retained in the Anglican rite. Here Hooker invokes a highly traditional argument concerning the divinely appointed end or goal of matrimony, namely the replenishing of the earth with blessed inhabitants and ultimately of heaven with saints. If the having and bringing up of children is the goal, the means requires the 'subalternation' of women to men. This is naturally grounded upon the inequality of the sexes, 'because thinges equall in everie respect are never willinglie directed one by another'. Woman is thus not merely brought into being after man, but is 'inferior in excellencie' to him. Thus the delivering up of the woman by her father is one of the customs which have a true and sufficient reason, rooted as it is in the ancient authority of husband, father or tutor over all women. The ceremony accordingly reminds women 'of a dutie whereunto the verie imbecillitie of theire

nature and sex doth bind them, namelie to be allwaies directed
guided and ordered by others, although our positive lawes doe not
tie them now as pupils'.[12]

IV

These uncompromising expressions of female subordination to male
power are, nonetheless, utterly incidental to the course of Hooker's
argument. He is apparently not in the least interested in the
theoretical questions about the status of women which had already
surfaced in European discussion.[13] Hooker is a traditionalist for
whom no serious question arises which might lead him to place
women in any other position than that accorded her in the standard
theory. The subordination of women was integral to that theory,
as it was for most leading Roman Catholic and Protestant writers
of the age.

   It is essential to the argument of this paper to note the interlocking
character of the disciplines whose arguments contributed to the
theory of female inferiority. This theory was composed of a variety
of elements from law, philosophy, ethics and medicine as well as
from theology, as Ian Maclean's most impressive treatment of the
theme has demonstrated.[14] One example will suffice. Hooker's
reference, noted above, to women's 'imbecillitie' is not a gratuitous
insult, but a standard piece of legal theory deriving from the *Digest*,
where woman's disbarment from succession, office and privilege,
the legal consequence of her *deterior conditio*, is justified by her alleged
levitas, *fragilitas*, *imbecillitas* and *infirmitas*.[15] The French jurist,
André Tiraqueau, compiled in his seminal treatise on marriage law
a list of occurrences of these words in Roman Law. But the work
itself is full of references to theology, medicine, ethics and ancient
literature, as well as to law, all in support of female inferiority.[16]
The marriage of Aristotle's anatomical and ethical theories to the
patristic understanding of the creation and fall had contrived to
produce a synthesis according to which woman was an incomplete
version of the male (a *mas occasionatus*).[17] Her weaker powers of
reason are the grounds for her being deceived, this explanation
cohering with the *deterior conditio* of woman in law.[18] Maclean
describes the relationship between the disciplines as 'molecular' as

well as 'hierarchical'. [19] Thus although Aristotelian medical theory provides a basis for morality, and medicine and ethics underlie law, the synthesis of Aristotelian and Christian theses is full of ambiguities, apparent and real contradictions and open possibilities which make it responsive to slow change. Hooker's participation in the synthesis was total, informing every aspect of his minimal references to women. But he wrote at a time when for the first time the scholastic synthesis came under attack as a whole. And his significance is that he provides the Church with a way of understanding what it might mean to come to new terms with the new view of woman which was shortly to develop in modern Europe.

The case that can be argued in this connection rests on Hooker's awareness that certain aspects of church law can properly vary with time and place. But it is important not to overstate the point. His thought is permeated with Aristotelian assumptions and there is nothing to suggest a willingness in him to entertain in relation to the place of women even contemporary ideas which conflicted with the scholastic synthesis. As we have seen in Hooker's treatment of marriage the necessity of a relationship of superiority/inferiority, which is ultimately derived from Aristotle's dualities, is simply assumed as axiomatic. Although we now have been forced to separate Aristotle's ethics from his physics in order to give any kind of future for Aristelian thought at all, [20] Hooker could not have envisioned how this could be done. The most that can be said is that just as our treatment of Aristotle is likely to be eclectic, so was Hooker's though in different proportion; it is perhaps relevant to add that we are no more obliged to accept or reject Hooker's scholasticism *in toto*, than Hooker was to adopt Aristotle's entire political philosophy.

V

The issue, then, that we have to investigate is Hooker's approach to church polity. As is well known, he adopted from Jewel, Whitgift and other Anglican writers the distinction between things necessary to salvation and matters indifferent. [21] It was already conventional Lutheran apologetic that rites and ceremonies belonged to matters indifferent. Hooker agreed, and it is the purpose of Book III of the

Laws to carry his point against the Puritans, who, he holds, insist that discipline and church government belong to things necessary to salvation.

Hooker's position as it unfolds is differentiated and subtle. Although at first sight it looks as though he is going to argue quite simply that what he prefers to call 'church-politie'[22] is a matter of indifference to be decided by each national or regional body for itself, by means of a fundamental analysis of different types of law he shows to what extent the Church must rely on Scripture and to what extent and how she must develop her own positive regulations. In chapters 1-4 of Book III all that is in mind is the sharp distinction, which he needs for polemical purposes, between what he calls 'the verie essence of Christianitie' (the earliest use in English known to me of this phrase), by which he means one Lord, one faith, and one baptism,[23] and ceremonies, such as marrying with a ring, the use of the sign of the cross at baptism, kneeling at the Eucharist and so forth.[24] From ceremonies are excepted 'Sacramentes, or anie other the like substantiall duties in the exercise of religion'.[25]

In chapter 5 Hooker turns his attention to the Puritan use of the phrase 'commanded by the word of God', and asks the pertinent question, What is the proper use of Scripture?

> When that which the word of God doth but deliver historically, wee conster without any warrant as if it were legally meant, and so urge it further then wee can proove that it was intended, doe we not adde to the lawes of God, and make them in number seeme moe then they are?[26]

The argument is plainly *ad hominem*, in that it represents the Puritans as multiplying 'lawes' without due grounds, the very charge they brought against the conformists. But we should note that the exegetical sensitivity which refuses to quote 'by-speeches in some historicall narration or other' as though they amounted to the 'most exact forme of lawe' is the precursor of a type of historical relativism.

'Commaunded by the word of God', then, is an inadequately refined tool for the proper use of Scripture, and Hooker uses this fact as a pretext for a general argument in favour of the use of reason in Scriptural interpretation. It is, he says, the Church which first instructs us to treat the Scripture as authoritative, which enquiry and experience then confirm. Reason in this context can both refute error and build up faith, aided and directed by the Holy Spirit. Reason, therefore, can also be used in the same context for the formulation of the laws of church polity. This is precisely the point which Hooker desires to make. No church polity is good unless God be the author of it. But God may be the author of it in two ways, either by supernatural revelation, or by the Holy Spirit's guided use of the natural light of reason ('those thinges which men finde out by helpe of that light, which God hath given them unto that ende').[27] Thus though Scripture itself contains many laws, there are a number of matters

> for which the scripture hath not provided by any law, but left them unto the carefull discretion of the Church; . . . and what is so in these cases, partely scripture and partly reason must teach to discerne.[28]

At this point Hooker brings to bear on his argument the analysis of the different types of law which he has already provided in Book I. The three types of law which concern this argument are the law of reason (which Hooker also calls the law of nature), the divine law revealed in the Scriptures, and human law. The last of these, which includes all church constitutions, is subject to the criterion of the former two.[29] The complicating factor is the evident fact that Scripture contains a variety of material, both precedents and examples, natural laws and 'positive laws'. The last are called positive, rather than human law, to signify the fact that their role is not merely to instruct, but to enjoin and constrain.[30] There are two kinds of 'positive' laws, those which are 'mixed' and which amount to the ratification of natural law, and those which are 'merely' positive, that is, are within the province of human societies to determine as seems convenient.[31] But, and here is the rub, it is not self-evident from Scripture itself which kind of material is which.

> When scripture doth yeelde us precedents, how far forth they are to bee followed; when it giveth naturall lawes, what particular

order is thereunto most agreeable; when positive, which waye
to make lawes unrepugnant unto them; yea though all these
shoulde want, yet what kind of ordinances woulde be moste for
that good of the Church which is aimed at, al this must be by
reason founde out.[32]

Church polity is the area of 'positive law', but it is not, for that
reason, arbitrary or, in the modern sense, a matter of indifference.
But positive law is mutable, and Hooker is at pains to do justice
to the complexity of this issue. The mere fact that a law is given
in Scripture is not itself a decisive consideration. Sometimes positive
law is given with an indication as to how long it is to remain in
force. But if not, we can only judge the question of whether change
is permissible or not by considering 'the ende for which it was made,
and by the aptnese of thinges therein prescribed unto the same
end'.[33] The three types of Jewish laws show these principles at
work. The *moral* law is unchanged because the matter of it continues
as before, the *ceremonial* law is at an end because, although the matter
continues, the end or purpose has ceased; the *judicial* law is mutable,
because though the end continues, yet the matter is in some respects
altered.[34]

By these means Hooker reaches the paradoxical sounding
conclusion that

> God never ordeyned any thing that could be bettered. Yet many
> things he hath that have bene chaunged, and that for the better.
> That which succeedeth as better now when change is requisite,
> had bene worse when that which now is chaunged was instituted.
> Otherwise God had not then left this to choose that, neither would
> now reject that to choose this, were it not for some new growne
> occasion making that which hath bene better worse. In this case
> therefore men doe not presume to chaunge God's ordinance, but
> they yeelde thereunto requiring it selfe to be chaunged.[35]

The importance of this principle of change for our argument is
obvious. According to it, it may be agreed that the restriction of
the priesthood to males at one time was the ordinance of God. But
at some 'new growne occasion' that same positive law may become

the worse course for the Church to follow. The fact that the first law was indeed the law of God, and given by his authority, by no means demonstrates its unchangeableness.[36] The question would be whether or not the positive law given in the Scriptures had such a connection to natural law that its maintenance did not acquire the extra force of universality. But whether that is so or not, would, on Hooker's own argument, be a matter for reason itself to determine.

How would Hooker himself have interpreted the question of the ordination of women to the priesthood? The answer is hardly in doubt, and precisely illustrates his method of argument. The idea that women would be 'teachers in the house of God', he holds, as we have seen, to be 'a gross absurdity' in the light of the apostolic injunctions. This would be, in other words, an instance of Scripture giving a clear positive law. Moreover, for Hooker, such a law would undoubtedly have been a case of 'mixed' positive law, since natural reason also taught women's inferiority. Such at least is clear from his traditional handling of the place of women in marriage, which closely follows the terms of the scholastic synthesis. But if Hooker's own position on the question, had it occurred to him to raise it, cannot be in doubt, neither can the fact that it was being undermined, even as he wrote, by the fact of the rule of Queen Elizabeth, whose supremacy in the Church as monarch was likewise a matter of positive law. Hooker must surely have known of the fierce debate about the propriety of the government of women such as not merely Elizabeth I, but also Catherine de Médicis and Mary, Queen of Scots.[37] He can scarcely have been ignorant of the argument produced in 1588 by an Oxford scholar, John Case, in favour of feminine rule where the ability is present, and denying that the distinctively feminine humours adversely affect the mind.[38] He lived at a time when the Aristotelian doctrine of inherent female inferiority, rooted in logic and physiology, was already proving itself to be impermanent.

VI

But what of the question of ordination? Was that, too, for Hooker a matter of positive law, or was it a sacrament covered by the faith content of the Gospel? Although Hooker does not give ordination the explicit title of a sacrament, he sings a paean of praise to the authority and power of the ministry, which God alone can bestow.[39] By the time he came to write Book V, Hooker had come to accept the doctrine which was relatively new to Anglican apologetic that the origins of episcopacy lay in the distinction which Christ had made between the Twelve and the Seventy.[40] This had been argued by Hadrian de Saravia in his *De Diversis Ministrorum Evangelii Gradibus* of 1590, and it proved increasingly attractive to many Anglicans (including Hooker) in place of the Jeromian theory held by most Elizabethan divines that episcopacy was first introduced after the death of the Apostles.[41] But he makes abundantly clear that his argument does not depend on the former view, since we may claim the ministry to be of divine origin even if it be of human institution, provided that it has divine approbation.[42]

It is, therefore, quite consistent with Hooker's basic theory for him to say that there are conditions under which it would be legitimate to vary the form of church polity. The Tractarians found it a difficult passage to swallow, and Anglo-Catholics have choked on it ever since, but it is plain enough. Compared with matters necessary to salvation, the scriptures are not so insistent or clear on matters relating to ecclesiastical polity that 'much which it hath taught [might] become unrequisite, sometimes because we need not use it, sometimes also because we cannot'.[43] Then follows the admission that the failure of the reformed Churches of France and Scotland to retain episcopacy, though a defect, could not be considered a cause of serious reproach or blame. This is a clear example of Hooker's readiness to judge of times and seasons.

A similar interpretation can be given to Hooker's discussion of the Jeromian theory. Even if it is by custom that bishops hold authority in the Church, none the less what has long continued in the Church without alteration is an integral part of its being considered a divine institution. The conclusion is that the power of bishops may be taken away if their behaviour becomes 'proud, tyrannical and unreformable'.[44] For Hooker, ever sensitive to the exigencies of history, the whole body of the Church hath power to alter, with general consent and upon necessary occasions, even the positive laws of the apostles, if there be no command to the contrary, and it manifestly appears to her, that change of times have clearly taken away the very reasons of God's first institution.[45]

Likewise in particular emergencies the church may ordain someone where there is no bishop who could do so.

We are not simply without exception to urge a lineal descent of power from the Apostles by continued succession of bishops in every effectual ordination.[46]

In these exceptional cases, and Hooker, we should note, draws their conditions very tightly, the crucial factor is the consent of the Church. Hooker did not believe in episcopal government of the Church, nor even in clerical government. The power of the government, he lays down in Book I, apart from the consent of the governed is no better than tyranny, and a principle he applies to both Church and State.[47] It is for this reason that he gives Parliament as well as Convocation a role in the making of ecclesiastical law. Hooker by no means anticipated the secularisation of the Church; as Cargill Thompson pertinently observes, 'had he done so, he would hardly have approved of the continued survival of Parliament's right to make laws for the Church'.[48] But it cannot seriously be doubted that he would have regarded the participation of the laity in synodical government as a normal and desirable state of affairs, conducive to that testing of consent without which no form of government is secure.

Nothing in Hooker's treatment of ordination would lead us to the conclusion that it could be an area of church polity exempt from the general considerations relating to positive law which he advanced. He anticipates the fact that different contexts will give rise to different decisions, and this he labels an 'harmonious dissimilitude'.[49] What is permanent in the ministry is the task of teaching the Gospel of Christ.

As an example of what may properly be considered a temporary measure he instances Paul's instructions to Timothy concerning the

choice of widows (1 Tim. 5.9). God's clergy are a permanent state
to carry out the laws governing the administration of the word and
sacraments. To this necessity he adds the hierarchical distinction of
degrees among the clergy so as to secure order, and the necessity
of ordination. The rest are matters on which the Church has the
right to make positive law in accordance with scriptural principles
and right reason.

The point of this enquiry is that it shows Hooker to be the architect
of an understanding of church polity which can seriously consider
the necessity of change, even in an institution as traditional as an
all-male priesthood. It does not, of course, turn Hooker into an
advocate of women's ordination. But on his own principles Hooker
would undoubtedly have been ready to consider an argument which
destroyed the status of the doctrine of women's subordination as a
deliverance of natural reason. The point can be made more precisely.
The issue is not patriarchy (the rule of the father in the household),
but male dominance. Aristotelian physiology and psychology are
entirely general in their application to womankind, and are the basis
upon which the impropriety of female dominance can be urged. Once
this generalised basis was abandoned (and it must be said to have
lingered in psychology long into the twentieth century), the support
from 'natural reason', essential to Hooker's prescription for a mixed
positive law, evaporates. When generalised female subordination
ceases to make sense medically or empirically, the route must be open
for a reappraisal of the scriptural positive law concerning the
impropriety of female teachers.

This is not merely a matter of the ordination of women. A
consistent modern application of the scholastic synthesis would be
such as to preclude the participation of women in *any* form of public
office or leadership role. Those who urge the Church's tradition as
an argument against women's ordination are inconsistent with that
tradition in failing to deplore female monarchs, prime ministers,
members of parliament or members of church synods, heads of
church colleges, and chairpersons of bodies of great power in State
and Church. To have capitulated in this arena in order to preserve
a *cordon sanitaire* around the Church's ministry is absolutely to have
abandoned Hooker's position.

What we discover, then, in Hooker is an undeniably Anglican

doctrine of the Church which enables us to reflect seriously upon the implications for church polity of the new understanding of the female–male relationship. It is a position which has no obligation to be unremittingly hostile to the church tradition in order to satisfy the instincts of radical feminism, nor, on the other hand, is it obliged to assume the immutability of laws even of divine origin. It is a position, moreover, which has a high doctrine of the apostolic ministry, and no *a priori* objection to the existence of a hierarchy. It would not feel obliged to impose the same structures upon all cultures at the same time, and could enjoy what Hooker describes in a felicitous phrase as the 'manifold and yet harmonious dissimilitude of those wayes whereby his Church upon earth is guided from age to age'.[50]

With these considerations in mind one may return to the question of the official response of the Roman Catholic Church. The documents, both the Declaration and the Commentary, seem plainly of a provisional character, striving both to start and end on a positive note, though conscious of the apparent negativity of their central teaching. The Declaration, *Inter insigniores*, recalls the opposition of the Second Vatican Council to discrimination based upon sex. The Commentary notes that it would have been desirable to have inserted into the Declaration a more general presentation on the question of the advancement of women; but, it adds, 'the time is not ripe for such a comprehensive exposition, because of the research and work in progress on all sides'.[51] But both publications are characterised by an extreme reluctance to present an historical picture of the traditional scholastic synthesis, claiming that the 'undeniable influence of prejudices unfavourable to women' or the presence of arguments 'that modern thought would have difficulty in admitting or would even rightly reject' can be easily separated from the Church's constant tradition.[52] One can have no such confidence.[53] So long as the status accorded to women remains in doubt, the isolation of the Church's priesthood from a general theory of the natural relations of the sexes strikes the reader as defensive, and in a strict sense uncatholic.

The argument of this paper brings one to the point where, without denying what the Church has maintained in the past or imposing an unhistorical interpretation upon it, an Anglican can freely face the challenge of recapturing the vision of a 'discipleship of equals', which is also part of the scriptural portrait of the nature of the Church. It may be that this vision could not have survived the Church's inculturation in the Graeco-Roman world, in which it was only wealthy widows who could exercise any kind of leadership through patronage. The self-interested character of the male medical science which asserted the natural imbecility of women can readily be recognised, and even excused. Equality, even in the Church, has little currency value until women acquired equal access to education and wives freedom from the burden of involuntary pregnancy. A new-grown occasion is upon us, and Richard Hooker provides us with the fundamental equipment with which to face it.

NOTES

1. *Laws* III, xi, 8. Quotations from Hooker are from the Folger Library Edition of his works (Harvard University Press, Cambridge, Mass, 1977–).

2. *Woman and the Priesthood*, Declaration on the Question of the Admission of Women to the Ministerial Priesthood, Sacred Congregation for the Doctrine of the Faith (Vatican City, 1977), p. 11.

3. The obvious candidates, Geneva or Wittenberg, identify the brand of Protestantism too closely. Perhaps we should suggest Marburg, on account of cacophony of squabbling Protestant voices to be heard at the Colloquy (1529), and therefore conforming to this kind of Anglican prejudice.

4. See S. W. Sykes, 'Have Anglicans no special doctrines of their own?', *The Franciscan*, Vol. XXX, No. 1, Jan. 1988, pp. 32–7.

5. By Peter Lake in his *Moderate Puritans and the Elizabethan Church* (Cambridge, 1982).

6. On which see Louis B. Wright, *Middle Class Culture in Elizabethan England* (Chapel Hill, N. Carolina, 1935), ch. xiii, 'The Popular Controversy over Woman'; Ruth Kelso, *Doctrine for the Lady of the Renaissance* (Urbana, Illinois, 1956), esp. ch. 2, 'Women in the Scheme of Things'; Ian Maclean, *The Renaissance Notion of Women* (Cambridge, 1980); Simon Shepherd, *Amazons and Warrior Women* (Brighton, 1981); Linda Woodbridge, *Women and the English Renaissance, Literature and the Nature of Womankind 1540–1610* (Brighton, 1984); and Lisa Jardine,

Still Harping on Daughters: Women and Drama in the Age of Shakespeare (Brighton, 1983).

7. *Laws* I, xv, 2.

8. Preface iii, 13. This coheres with Thomas Aquinas' opinion that the natural piety of women is not a particular mental attribute, but a lack (a *defectus contemplationis*) resulting in a tendency toward credulity (*Summa Theologica* 2a 2ae 83, 3). That there were both gains and losses to women in the Protestant Reformation is nicely argued by N. Z. Davis, in her essay 'City Women and Religious Change', *Society and Culture in Early Modern France* (Stanford, California, 1975), pp. 65–95.

9. *Laws*, Preface iii, 13. The more independent role of women in the Puritan movement has frequently attracted comment. See 'Women and Puritanism', ch. 5 of Shepherd, *Amazons*.

10. See Calvin's *Institutes*, 4, 15, 20 and Bullinger's *Decades* (Parker Society 4) pp. 370–72; as noted by John E. Booty in Vol. 4 of Folger Library edition of the *Laws* (Cambridge, Mass, 1982), pp. 209–10.

11. *Laws* V, lxii, 1–3, and 22. In the last paragraph of this chapter Hooker refers to 'divers reformed Churches' which do allow women to baptise in cases of necessity. These, doubtless, would be Lutheran churches, perhaps those of Hesse and Brandenberg-Nuremberg. So Booty, op. cit., p. 210.

12. *Laws* V, lxxiii, 1–5. It should be added that Calvin had also asserted the need for the wife to be subject to the husband, in order to guarantee the subordination of both to the authority of God (*Commentary on the Epistles of Paul the Apostle to the Corinthians* (Edinburgh, 1900), pp. 232f.

13. Henry Cornelius Agrippa's *De nobilitate et praecellentia foeminei sexus . . . declamatio* (1529: E. T. *A treatise of the nobility and excellency of womankind*, London, 1542) is an example. But its radicalism is usually interpreted as an exercise in rhetoric, perhaps because the idea of women's equality could be treated in no other way. See Maclean, *Renaissance Notion of Women*, pp. 80 and 91.

14. See note 6 above.

15. The main passage relevant to women's legal status reads as follows: 'Women are excluded from all civil and public offices; and thus they may not be *judices*, nor magistrates, nor advocates; nor may they intervene on another's behalf in law, nor act as agents' (*De regulis juris antiqui*, 50, 16, 2). In a volume published in Lyons in 1593, five eminent scholars comment on the position of women in Roman, Holy Roman and Canon Law, and references to the *imbecillitas* of women are frequent. Cf. 1. Maclean, *Women Triumphant, Feminism in French Literature, 1610–1652* (Oxford, 1977), pp. 13ff.

16. *De Legibus connubialibus* (1513) I, 1, 70–6 in *Opera omnia* II, 15–17, discussed by Maclean, *Renaissance Notion of Women*, pp. 3 and 83.

17. Maclean, op. cit., pp. 8f., referring to Thomas Aquinas, *Summa Theologica* 1a, 92, 1.

18. Maclean, op. cit., p. 15, referring to Peter Lombard, *Sententiae* II, 20 and Thomas Aquinas, *Summa Theologica* 2a 2ae, 163,4, and 165,2.

19. Maclean, op. cit., p. 83.

20. Here one thinks primarily in modern times of Alasdair MacIntyre's powerful argument in *After Virtue* (London, 1981).

21. For what follows I am especially indebted to the lucid analysis of Hooker's political philosophy in W. D. J. Cargill Thompson's essay 'The Philosopher of the "Politic Society": Richard Hooker as a Political Thinker', in his (posthumous) *Studies in the Reformation*, ed. C. W. Dugmore (London, 1980), pp. 131–91.

22. For the interesting and significant reason that it lays too much weight on 'the exercise of superiority peculiar unto rulers and guides of others', *Laws* III, i, 14.

23. *Laws* III, i, 4. On the history of this term see H. Wagenhammer, *Das Wesen des Christenums* (Mainz, 1973) and S. W. Sykes, *The Identity of Christianity* (London, 1984), esp. pp. 211–38 and 250–61.

24. Other examples are given in *Laws* III, v. 1.

25. *Laws* III, iii, 4.

26. *Laws* III, v. 1.

27. *Laws* III, ii, 1.

28. *Laws* III, ix, 1.

29. 'All our controversie in this cause concerning the orders of the Church is, what particulars the Church may appoint. That which doth finde them out is the force of man's reason. That which doth guide and direct his reason is first the generall law of nature, which law of nature and the morall law of Scripture are in the substance of law all one', *Laws* III, ix, 2.

30. *Laws* I, x, 8.

31. *Laws* I, x, 10.

32. *Laws* III, ix, 1.

33. *Laws* III, x, 1.

34. *Laws* III, x, 4.

35. *Laws* III, x, 5.

36. 'I therefore conclude that nether God's being author of laws for government of his Church, nor his committing them unto Scripture, is any reason sufficient wherefore all churches should for ever be bounde to keepe them without chaunge', *Laws* III, x, 7.

37. See Maclean, *Feminism in French Literature*, p. 58.

38. 'Nature often makes woman shrewd, hard work makes her learned, upbringing makes her pious, and experience makes her wise. What, therefore, prevents women from playing a full part in public affairs? If one is born free, why should she obey? If one is heiress to a kingdom, why should she not reign? Divine law, the history of nations, ancient insitutions, and examples drawn from Holy Writ all support such arguments', *Sphaera civitatis* (Oxford, 1588, I, 3, p. 33; cited in

Maclean, *The Renaissance Notion of Women*, p. 61 (Latin, p. 95).

39. *Laws* V, lxxvii.
40. *Laws* V, lxxviii, 5. See W. D. J. Cargill Thompson's discussion in 'Anthony Marten and the Elizabethan Debate on Episcopacy' in G. V. Bennett and J. D. Walsh (eds.), *Essays in Modern English Church History in Memory of Norman Sykes* (London, 1966), pp. 44–75.
41. Hooker acknowledges his conversion to the new theory in *Laws* VII, xi, 8.
42. *Laws* VII, xi, 10.
43. *Laws* III, xi, 16.
44. *Laws* VII, v, 8.
45. *Laws* VII, v, 8.
46. *Laws* VII, xiv, 11.
47. *Laws* I, x, 8.
48. 'The Philosopher of the "Politic Society" ', p. 190.
49. *Laws* III, xi, 8.
50. *Laws* III, xi, 8.
51. *The Ordination of Women*, Circumstances and Origin of the Declaration Women and the Priesthood (Catholic Truth Society, Do. 494; London, nd), p. 4.
52. *Women and the Priesthood*, pp. 5–6.
53. Indeed in one place the Commentary leaves wholly ambiguous whether or not the proposition of St Thomas Aquinas that *mulier est in statu subjectionis* is 'scarcely defensible' or the direct (and presumably defensible) exegesis of the first chapters of Genesis and 1 Timothy 2.12–14.

9

The Status of Woman
in the Thought of Karl Barth

Paul S. Fiddes

At the assembly of the World Council of Churches in Amsterdam, in 1948, Karl Barth spent every afternoon chairing a committee on 'The Life and Work of Women in the Church'. In a letter written at the time Barth records his impression of this occasion, regretting his failure to convince the women present that: '. . . besides writing Galatians 3.28 (which was about the one thing that they joyfully affirmed), Paul also said several other things on the relation between men and women which were important and right'.[1]

Without doubt, one of the texts to which Barth must have drawn their attention was 1 Corinthians 11.3, since he gives extended attention to it in several places in his *Church Dogmatics*: 'While every man has Christ for his head, woman's head is man, as Christ's head is God.' [2] It is apt to begin our enquiry into Barth's thought on the status of women with his exegesis of this text, not only because it provides us with a direct way into his convictions on the theme, but also because it hints at some open-endedness in his thinking. As so often with Barth, although he is constructing a complete theological system which appears on the surface to be a seamless garment of tight argument, in fact he leaves loose ends which his readers may knit up into new patterns.

1. The Covenant Relationship

In his discussion of Paul's sentence in 1 Corinthians 11.3, Barth makes the central point that Paul is not presenting a hierarchy of headship, as if there were a *chain* of subordination stretching from God the Father, to God the Son, to man and finally to woman (at the bottom of the pecking order). He observes that the apparently untidy order in which man, Christ, woman and God are mentioned makes clear that they are not being arranged in a scale: 'They contain neither deduction from above downwards nor induction from below upwards.'[3] This is not a hierarchy at all, but a comparison of sets of relationships – God with Christ, Christ with humankind and man with woman. To these three sets Barth adds the further one from a similar passage in Ephesians 5.22–3 – that between Christ and the Church. In the wider context of Barth's theology, these relationships are to be understood as covenants, and they stand in analogy to each other. The creaturely covenant relationship between man and woman is part of the covenant between human beings in general; this reflects the covenant between Jesus Christ and human beings, which is modelled on the covenant between God and the man Jesus, which is finally an image of the eternal covenant between the Father and the Son in the love of the Spirit.[4] In the last resort, then, Barth dares to say that the personal relationship between male and female is an image of the relations between the Persons of the Trinity.[5]

Of course, there is no possibility, in Barth's view, that these correspondences might be 'analogies of being' in the sense of classical theology. Though Barth does not always seem to understand what the scholastic theologians meant by an 'analogy of being',[6] he is emphatic that the human reason cannot discover these 'analogies of relation' for itself by reflecting upon the natural world; nor is there a graded ascent of levels of being linking God and humanity. For Barth, there is an infinite difference between Creator and creature, and the human mind can have no knowledge of God based upon human experience; all that is known of God must be revealed to human beings by God himself, through his Word. Rather, these analogies are 'analogies of grace', set up by God's free and gracious decision; they are also 'analogies of faith', which are revealed by God, and which in themselves offer no way into a knowledge of God.[7] We shall be returning to this theology of the Word of God in a moment.

In this text, then, Barth perceives not a 'ladder' of subordination, but a parallel series of I-Thou relationships. There is no question, for instance, of woman having access to God through man as her mediator.[8] Nor is there any implied domination, with ascending levels of power, as if man is to rule woman as God rules the universe. Man and woman are equal before God in their creaturely existence; they stand in exactly the same relationship to the Creator and Redeemer of their lives.[9] They are also equal in the sense that they equally need each other; they can only truly *be* male and female through their orientation to each other. The male, for example, only discovers what maleness means in fellowship with woman; here Barth makes the suggestion that 'the very dubious masculine enterprise of war' would become intrinsically impossible if the male remembered that his encounter with woman was the norm for *all* human encounters.[10] In this passage in 1 Corinthians 11, Barth identifies the focal place of verse 11: 'in the Lord woman is not independent of man nor man of woman'.

However, the conclusion which Barth draws from the statements of verse 3 about headship, is that there is an area in which man and woman are *not* equal; they are not equal in the order of function which God has allotted to them. It is the place of woman to be subordinate and submissive to man, and this is made clear by the analogy of covenants. As the Father comes before the Son in order of origin in the Godhead, and as the Triune God comes before the world, so man comes before woman.[11] The story of creation in Genesis 2, in which woman is taken out of man, portrays this truth of divine ordering. The man comes 'before' woman in the sense that he 'takes the lead as the inspirer, leader and initiator in their common being and action'.[12] Conversely, as the Son is obedient to the Father, the creature to Creator, and the Christian community to Christ, so the woman is to submit to man, in the sense that she follows the initiative he takes. Barth works very hard at showing that this superordination of man is nothing to do with exaltation, superiority or oppression; it is merely a matter of function. Each partner is equally free, and equally honoured, in his or her own task.

Woman does not come short of man in any way, nor renounce her right, dignity and honour, nor make any surrender, when theoretically and practically she recognises that in order she is woman, and therefore [not A but] B and therefore behind and subordinate to man . . . that she is ordered, related and directed to man and thus has to follow the initiative which he must take.[13]

Such a difference in function does not glorify the status of man over woman, according to Barth, or give the male any right to oppress the female. He finds the controlling thought in the passage from Ephesians 5 to be the verse commanding husband and wife to be 'subject to one another out of reverence to Christ' (5.21); this he understands to be the principle that each should give what is due to the other because of the task assigned them. It has, he comments, 'nothing to do with patriarchalism, or with a hierarchy of domestic and civil values and powers'.[14]

Neither, Barth asserts, can this functional difference be founded upon any different gender characteristics which might bind men and women to certain vocations. Barth rejects a typology of the sexes, such as the view that man is the natural leader because of his hunting and aggressive instincts, and that the woman is the natural follower because of her guarding and tending instincts.[15] In rejecting these typologies, Barth comes surprisingly close to one strand in the modern feminist movement, which regards attempts to identify gender differences as cultural stereotyping. There is a strong (though not universal) feminist opinion that all so-called feminine aspects of the human personality are gender roles created by a male, patriarchal culture, and are part of the oppression of women by men.[16] It is men who have turned biological, or reproductive, differences into gender differences in order to subordinate women and limit their opportunities. ('The woman's place is in the home', 'not a suitable job for a woman', and so on.) While radical feminists reject gender differences altogether, Barth's point is that such characteristics, together with different functions, are called into being by the divine command. In Barth's view, the woman is submissive because God has called her to this vocation, not because she has certain natural qualities which suit her for it. Indeed, Barth has such a high view of the freedom of God's word that he believes the call to men and women to be true to their sex may take new and surprising forms, 'right outside the systems in which we like to think'.[17] This is one of those open ends in Barth's thought that I want to take up later.

Basically, however, Barth is an eloquent advocate of the case for woman as 'submissive but equal', or 'subordinate in function but not in dignity'. This is a common approach to the question of women's rights and status in the Church today, and for myself I affirm that I share the feeling of many women that they are being condescended to, when it is urged that following the leadership of men in the family or in the Church does not make them any less equal or less free, but only *different* in their vocation.[18] If we agree with Barth that the covenant idea does present the partners as having a difference of function (and I certainly want to argue this), nevertheless we may still question whether the functional difference has to include the elements of subordination and superordination. We might well ask, with the women at the Amsterdam conference, whether the insight of Paul at least in Galatians 3.28 is not more radical than this: 'In Christ Jesus there is no such thing as Jew and Greek, slave and freeman, male and female.' In fact, Barth himself hints at other ways ahead, and we can see this most clearly if we take two key points in his exposition of the human and divine covenant relationships, as they are revealed in the text of 1 Corinthians 11.3. We must first consider more exactly the way that Barth tries to defend the dignity and freedom of woman in her role, and second we must reflect further on the Trinity as an image of human partnership.

2. The honour of woman's service

Barth claims, as we have seen, that the subordination of women to male leadership is not an inferior status. It is a place of great honour. In the first place, this is because the vocations of men and women must be understood to be 'in Christ'. Barth plucks this phrase from Paul, and not least from the passage in 1 Corinthians 11 we have been discussing. Christ is the centre of the whole argument. The subordination and superordination, leading and following, which women and men exercise belong to Christ himself; men and women only represent these aspects. If the role of the woman is compared to Christ in his obedience and humiliation before his Father ('Christ's head is God'), in accepting the role of suffering unto death, then we find both exaltation *and* lowliness in Christ. Christ is 'the sum of all subordination and stands relatively much lower than woman under man', just as he is the sum of all superordination.[19] Woman only represents the submission of Christ, as the man only represents his cosmic leadership. So male and female functions are not a matter of 'greater or less', for they are 'the affair of Christ'; man and woman thus have equal honour in being assigned these roles. Correspondingly, they are both equally obedient to Christ in taking these roles up. In submitting to male leadership and initiative, the woman is not obeying the man; she is obeying Christ, or the order which God has established in Christ. Likewise the man is obedient in taking up the task of being submitted to. There is no question of ruling or oppressing here. Thus when we turn to the analogy between Christ and his Church (Ephesians 5.22–3) we find Barth stressing that the husband as 'head' of the wife must love her with the same humble self-giving love with which Christ loved the Church.[20]

A second point made by Barth leads on from this first one. If we consider the analogy of headship between Christ and his Father, then we find that the humility of Christ is in harmony with his majesty, not in contradiction of it. A fundamental feature of Barth's Christology is his assertion that Christ is most divine in his lowly and suffering humanity; if we want to know the true nature of divinity then we do not begin with preconceived notions of a universal ruler. These are human and idolatrous ideas; we begin where God has actually revealed himself, in the stable at Bethlehem and the cross at Calvary. This is what divinity is like; in Christ Lordship and Service are the same final word.[21] The humanity of Christ is the humanity of God. If we protest that God cannot be limited and conditioned by his world and face death for our sake, then we are simply showing our pagan preconceptions; God is free to be and to do all this.[22] Thus, for woman to represent the humility and service of Christ is in fact to represent his divine Majesty. It is the eternal glory of Christ, his true divinity, to be obedient to the Father.

Barth's third argument for the honour of woman's service is based on the analogy between Christ and his Church. The Church is the human community which listens to the word of God; for humankind becomes truly human when it is the hearer and receiver of the word. In this it simply receives a gift, for there is nothing in the human mind that can make it capable of hearing the word. We cannot hear the word, and yet we *do* hear by a miracle of God's grace; we cannot speak the word back to God, and yet we *must*.[23] Now, the prime New Testament example of the receiver of the word is Mary the Mother of Jesus, and as such she is the prototype of all true humanity. The virgin birth, Barth explains, is a sign of pure receptivity; in face of the creative activity of God, the whole human race is *virgo*, that is: '. . . in the form of non-willing, non-achieving, non-creative, non-sovereign man, only in the form of man who can merely receive, merely be ready, merely let something be done to and with himself'.[24]

Not only Mary, but the whole of Mary's sex is in Barth's view a representative of this listener to the word, since Paul explicitly compares woman to the Christian community in drawing the analogy between husband as head of wife and Christ as head of the Church (Eph. 5.23). This means, concludes Barth, that woman actually has the honour of representing the redeemed community; 'the advantage of the wife, her birthright' (says Barth) is that she, not the man, attests the reality of the Church as it listens to Christ. If the wife fulfils her function in being submissive to her husband as the whole community is subordinate to Christ, then: '. . . the wife is not less but greater than her husband in the community. She is not the second but the first. In a qualified sense she is the community. The husband has no option but to order himself by the wife as she is subordinate in this way.'[25]

Barth adds that 'the curious wish of Schleiermacher that he had been a woman is not so foolish when seen against this background'. Elsewhere, Barth offers the interesting judgment on this nineteenth century theologian, that in his development of a theology of absolute dependence he had allowed the feminine aspects of his nature to outweigh the masculine. Barth says that he does not judge Schleiermacher for this, as 'there have always been far too many male or masculine theologians', and it makes Schleiermacher 'more interesting and lovable than the majority of those who despise him'.[26]

It would be hard to state better the case for the woman as 'submissive, but of equal honour': (a) the woman represents the humility of Christ, not her own; (b) this humility is in fact true glory; (c) the woman represents the whole Christian community. But I am, I confess, left very uneasy. There is a smack of masculine patronising about all this, as if the woman is to be persuaded, against her immediate reactions, that all is for the best when she admits the leadership and inspiration of man. In fact, I suggest that these very arguments may point in a rather different direction from the one which Barth intends.

(1) To begin with, if we take up Barth's description of woman as the archetypal hearer of the word of God in Christ, it would be unfair to conclude that Barth is simply placing the woman passively in the congregation of the Church, while the masculine clergy proclaim the word. This is a criticism made by one feminist theologian, Joan Romero, who complains that Barth is making the congregation take on a feminine role, 'passive and dependent'.[27] But Barth's point is that human beings can only witness to the divine word (Christ) in preaching, if they are themselves hearers of the word. It is the free act of God that he takes the human word and makes it a vehicle for the divine word, when the speaker is a listener. Barth does not only argue the need for passive receptivity in presence of the divine word; he urges a responsible speaking of the word which is required from human beings whose minds have been renewed by the Spirit. While we must not confuse the human word with the divine word, God only speaks his word (that is, unveils his very personality) through secular things such as human speech.[28] In the dialogue of the word, God calls human beings to return his own word to him.

Here again it seems to me that Joan Romero, with a proper concern about the subjection of women, has overplayed the 'master–servant' relation between God and humankind in Barth's thought. Barth believes that God *could* have been content to speak his word to himself, within the conversation partners of the Trinity, but as a matter of fact he has chosen to open out the circle of word and fellowship to creatures, and there is no going back on that eternal decision.[29] In the freedom of God to be what he chooses to be, he has chosen to include humanity within his own covenant life, as hearer *and* speaker of the word. The primordial decision of the Father, deep in eternity, is that the eternal Son should be identified with a human being, Jesus Christ. In determining his own manner of being as Son and Father in the fellowship of the Spirit, God also chooses *humankind*[30] and so takes the first step on his costly journey into the far country of the human world. So there is humanity in God, and a place for human speech.

Thus, the perfect hearer of the word is also the most responsible speaker of the word. And in Barth's view, Mary and all womankind are the archetypal listeners. One might say that Barth's logic would lead to the view that the best preacher would be a woman! This is rather in tension with his view that the woman's task is to follow the inspiration offered by the man, but here Barth's own theology may speak more truly than he imagines. In fact, Barth is rather cautious about drawing absolute rules from the rare injunctions in the New Testament that women should be silent in church, particularly in 1 Corinthians 14.34–5. Barth comments that the underlying principle here is that the command of God puts men and women in their proper place, but that this is a living command and not a dead law: so 'interpretations may vary as to where this place is, for the Lord is a living Lord and his command is ever new'. The essential point is that woman should always be woman, though 'it is undoubtedly the case that woman may also . . . speak in the assembly'.[31]

In this flexibility one may perhaps trace the results of mutual discussion between Barth and his secretary, assistant and companion in the great labour of the *Church Dogmatics*, the remarkable Charlotte Von Kirschbaum. In his exegesis of 1 Corinthians 11 Barth acknowledges that her own book, *The Real Woman* (1949) is 'along the same lines'. No doubt Barth understood their collaboration throughout the volumes of the *Dogmatics* from 1929 to 1965 as a matter of the woman's 'actualising the fellowship in which man can only precede her, stimulating, leading and inspiring'.[32] At any rate, in a lecture in 1951 entitled 'The Service of Woman in the Proclamation of the Word',[33] Von Kirschbaum builds a plea for the recognition of women ministers upon the Barthian argument of the woman as hearer of the word.

The implications of this argument reach, of course, beyond the question of women preachers, for Barth's whole view of humankind is as receiver of the divine word, which strikes at its existence and renews it. If the woman represents the true receiver of the word, one might think the logic to be that she would also be an initiator, inspirer and leader on the human scene.

(2) If it be protested that according to the series of analogies, it is still the man who represents Christ, who *is* the divine word, we notice that the terms of the analogies actually overlap. This is especially the case in Barth's presentation of the humble obedience of Christ, which is the centre point of his whole theology. In the comparison of husband and wife on the one hand, with Christ and his Church on the other, it is supposedly the wife who is to be submissive, representing the community. But, in dealing with the analogy of God as head of Christ, Barth rightly points out that there is no submission as utter and complete as that of Christ himself. No one else has been so abased. So from the perspective of one analogy it is the husband who is to represent the sacrificial and humble love of Christ, while from another it is the wife. The distinction between the submitting of the wife and the loving leadership of the man thus seems to have evaporated. It has been swallowed up in the glory and the humility of the cross. If we follow analogies of covenant, it is therefore an elusive task to try to allot the contrasting characteristics of Christ – his lordship and service, his divinity and humanity, his superordination and his subordination – to man and woman respectively. Barth tries to do this – 'His is the place of man, and His is the place of woman'.[34] But the very elusiveness of this placing ought to warn us that while human beings can bear the image of Christ as truly human, his attributes cannot be exclusively distributed between the sexes. This might in fact well lead us to a view of an overlap of true male and female qualities in men and women, a suggestion to which I want to return.

(3) But before that, there is a third point of expansion of Barth's argument about the honour of women. He is rightly troubled – even indignant – about the oppression of women by men. Since,

in his view, the submission of women is to the order of Christ, there should be no question of men lording it over women. Here he refers with approval to the work of Simone de Beauvoir, and her unmasking of the myth of the 'eternal feminine' by which man makes himself master of woman.[35] But the question therefore arises as to how the emancipation of woman which Barth desires can come about. He suggests that if women remain quietly submissive under the arrogance and injustice of men, this witness will win them to repentance. If the woman keeps her place in the divine order, and is not incited into disobedience, she will shame the man into returning to *his* obedience and his place.[36] This is also the strategy commended by Charlotte Von Kirschbaum in her study, but one is forced to doubt whether it is likely to succeed. If experience shows that it only confirms the oppression of women, one is bound to suspect this is a clue to a flaw in the whole argument. If men do not return to what Barth considers to be their proper place through the witness of the women who keep *their* place, one must ask whether the places have been rightly identified.

3. The image of the Trinity

We must return now to the analogy which Barth finds between the persons of the Trinity and human I-Thou relationships, typified in the male–female relationship. Barth finds a point of departure for this comparison in Genesis 1.27: 'in the image of God he created [man]; male and female he created them'. This Barth understands to mean that being created in the image of God consists *in* our human relationships as male and female.[37] Barth's argument is of course wider than comment on one text, finding a correspondence between the eternal covenant in which God freely determines his being as communion between Father and Son, and the covenant relationship between human persons in which they are free for each other. The consequent analogy between God as the head of Christ and man as the head of woman (1 Cor. 11.3) raises, however, some implications which Barth himself seems unwilling to recognise.

In his exposition of the doctrine of the Trinity, Barth employs the traditional idea of *perichoresis* or the total indwelling of each Person in the other.[38] The Persons mutually interpenetrate in their modes of being, so that God is one complex Personality, thrice the divine 'I', one God in threefold self-repetition.[39] This means, for instance, that while the Son is the 'elected' God because he is chosen to be identified with the man Jesus, he freely shares in that choice and so can also be called the 'electing' God.[40] So the Persons of the Trinity, although they are distinct, share their functions with each other. If the male–female relationship is an image of the Trinity, we might well ask whether the doctrine of God himself does not provide a basis for sharing of functions and vocations between men and women. If human personal relationships are a copy of the relationships within God, then ought we not to look for a kind of *perichoresis* in human sexuality?

Barth firmly answers no, but the way he says it leaves some open ends. Barth explains that there is an interchange of functions among the divine Persons because they make up One divine Personality: there are not three 'I's and three 'Lords' but one Lord and one divine I. Human persons do not make up one individual identity. Commenting further on Genesis 1.27, Barth therefore adds that there cannot be an *exact* analogy with human relationships.[41] The sexual difference is the sign of the creature, and humankind stands before God in the 'either/or' of male and female. Human beings must be obedient to God by affirming their sexual difference, and this for Barth includes the difference of function to which God has called them.

However, in Barth's own thought there is some reason for finding a closer analogy between the fellowship of the Trinity and human community than this. After all, while God is One Personality he cannot be *an* individual being; Barth affirms that the divine 'I' eternally repeats himself in three modes of being, and this prevents us from any idolatrous thoughts about God as an 'Ego' just like a human individual.[42] This divine 'I' is free to be Spirit and Son as well as Father, to be in relationship and not in solitude. Of course, the Persons of the Trinity do not differ in sex, but Barth insists they do differ in order of origin – the Father, for instance, does not exchange his fatherhood with the Son; yet this does not prevent their sharing their acts of love and creation in the world. From another angle, we see that the person in a human society also has open boundaries; to be a person is to live in encounter, in mutual participation, and not as a private individual. All this might incline us to look for some interchange of function and characteristics between men and women, a *perichoresis* having some analogy at least to the sharing within the Trinity.

Barth's profound perception into Genesis 1.27 is surely that the human *person* can only be understood in terms of a free giving and receiving within relationships, in the image of the divine Persons. Barth has moved too quickly from the concept of person to that of 'nature' when he finds the subordination of the divine Son mirrored in the human female gender; but he does rightly see that if the image of God is to do with personal relationships, it must have *some* relevance to the particular human relationship between the sexes. This, I suggest, would lead us to find a reflection of *perichoresis* as well as difference in the partnership of men and women.

Barth in fact distinguishes between two kinds of attempt that women might make to transcend their gender difference from men, to embark upon 'a flight from one's own sex'. On the one hand, the woman might try to deny any gender difference at all, beyond a mere reproductive specialisation (a biological fact which cannot be denied). She might quest for a 'neutral humanity' which is neither male nor female but simply human. She might reject the idea of any distinct feminine qualities and functions at all, as a trap laid by males to force her into conforming to their social stereotypes. Barth mentions Simone de Beauvoir as such a feminist, with her key phrase 'one is not born a woman, but one becomes it'.[43] Barth judges this to be a false reaction to male oppression, and a loss of humanity rather than a gaining of it. We ought to notice here that not all feminists agree that there are no distinct female qualities; some regret that male society has suppressed healthy female insights and approaches, and they prefer to live in women's communes where neglected qualities can flourish. In this alternative to male society, mutual creativity is to be fostered rather than competitiveness, intuition is to supplement (but not replace) argument, and the spirit of reconciliation overcomes possessiveness. If these admirable qualities are to emerge from a woman-centred culture, it does seem to be implied that they are somehow 'womanlike'. Of course, feminists will always insist that no jobs or vocations should be considered suitable or unsuitable for women on account of any presumed gender difference. Barth, as we have seen, agrees with that, but still maintains a difference of vocation based on something else – the divine command.

This brings us to the second way in which Barth finds women denying their sex and so their humanity, which is founded in the either/or of male and female. The female, he suggests, might attempt an exchange of vocation and role with the male – that is, might attempt to replace her vocation of following with his vocation of leading and inspiring. Here Barth returns to the incident described in 1 Corinthians 11 which sparked off Paul's text about headship; the women at Corinth were refusing to wear veils, and the issue here, as Barth sees it, is not the veils themselves but the fact that the women were not accepting their role as women. The veil was only the form in which the difference between male and female functions was expressed, and was really quite incidental in itself.[44] (It is, we might say, as incidental as the lost handkerchief in *Othello*.) As Barth reconstructs the affair, the women were 'in flight from their sex', and so from their humanity, perhaps misled by enthusiastic reports of what Paul had said in Galatians 3.28 about there being neither male nor female in Christ.

Here it seems to me that Barth's argument against role-sharing is not as strong as his argument against a neutralising of sex altogether. I mean this not only from the critic's point of view, but from what he himself has to say. In the first place, he readily admits that what the female (and male) vocation might *be* in any age and place is an open issue:

> The question what specific activity woman will claim and make her own as woman ought certainly to be posed in each specific case as it arises, not in the light of traditional misconceptions . . . Above all, woman herself ought not to allow the uncalled-for illusions of man, and his attempts to dictate what is suitable for her and what is not, to deter her from seriously and continually putting this question to herself.[45]

The form of the divine command will differ from age to age. One might then enquire of Barth whether in our age the divine command might be taking the form of an exchange of functions and a sharing of traditional roles. Such a radical extension of Barth's thought would be in line with the Apostle Paul himself if a widespread modern exegesis of 1 Corinthians 11 is correct. Several commentators interpret Paul as insisting upon women wearing a veil because it is the sign of their *own* authority to prophesy and pray, a mark of their new freedom in Christ.[46]

Another point Barth himself makes is that the meaning of what it is to be male and female only emerges in their mutual fellowship and encounter. We can have no totally preconceived ideas about the nature of the sexes until one defines the other. In accord with this, Barth's interpretation of the famous text of Galatians 3.28 is that 'The male is a male in the Lord only, but precisely, to the extent that he is with the female, and the female likewise.' Barth himself believes that this principle of reciprocity takes 'absolute precedence' over any difference in order between male and female.[47] We might then ask whether their vocations can be defined in advance in the way that Barth presumes to do; perhaps his description of the difference as lying between inspiring and following is just such a preconception.

If we accept Barth's insight into an analogy of covenant between male and female, God and man, divine Father and Son, then we are bound to agree that there are differences of function between men and women. But we might also conclude from a comparison with the Trinitarian doctrine of God that there is a mutual *sharing* of function and activity between them. The situation is, of course, a complicated one. A *perichoresis* or mutual interchange of functions and qualities cannot be simply deduced from the fact that male and female physiologies contain a blend of genetic materials of both sexes. No straight line can be drawn from a biological overlap to an overlap of either gender characteristics or social functions. The present debate about feminism has at least shown that while male and female qualities can be often 'felt' as present, it is nevertheless curiously difficult to define what they are, and that these characteristics are not simply divided between men and women but exist in different proportions within them.[48] The theologian Rosemary R. Ruether thus prefers to speak of a 'feminine way' of developing the personality and of integrating its component parts.[49] Similarly, no list of male and female functions can be simply read off from the analogy of the Trinity; Barth, as we have seen, makes too quick a leap from the obedience of the divine Son to a subordination of woman.

Barth's theology of covenant therefore leaves us with a direction and a quest. We have continually to discover what the particular functions of men and women might be, as these emerge in reciprocal relations. Such discovery will only come when women are given full access to all the jobs and vocations which are open to men, and when men take up the occupations that are often called 'women's work'. For we may take the clue from the image of the Trinity that the difference will lie in the mode of being of a person *within* the activity. Perhaps then we shall also discover those genuine male and female qualities which seem so elusive to define, and which have often been taken as an excuse for oppressing each other.

NOTES

1. Letter to Christopher Barth, *cit.* Eberhard Busch, *Karl Barth: his life from letters and autobiographical texts*, trans. J. Bowden (SCM Press, London, 1976), p. 358.
2. Translation from the New English Bible.
3. Karl Barth, *Church Dogmatics*, English Translation ed. G.W. Bromiley and T.F. Torrance (T. & T. Clark, Edinburgh, 1936–77), Vol. III, part 2, p. 311. Henceforth this work will be cited as *CD*, followed by volume number, part number and page. References to Vol. I/1 are to the Second Edition, trans. G.W. Bromiley, 1975.
4. See e.g. *CD* I/1, pp. 393–4; III/1, pp. 183–92; III/2, pp. 219 31, 319–24; IV/1, p. 203. For a concise summary of Barth's view of these analogies, see *Karl Barth's Table Talk*, Scottish Journal of Theology Occasional Papers 10, ed. J.D. Godsey (Edinburgh, 1963), p. 61.
5. *CD* III/1, pp. 195–6.
6. See the pertinent criticisms of Hans Urs Von Balthasar, *Karl Barth: Darstellung und Deutung Seiner Theologie* (Jacob Hegner, Cologne, 1956), especially pp. 175ff.
7. See e.g. *CD* I/1, p. 243–5, 457; III/2, pp. 220–22.
8. *CD* III/4, p. 173.
9. Ibid., p. 169; cf. III/2, pp. 310–11.

10. *CD* III/4, p. 168.
11. Ibid., pp. 173–4; III/2, pp. 311, 323–4; IV/1, pp. 202–3.
12. *CD* III/4, p. 170.
13. *CD* III/4, p. 171. Cf. ibid., p. 180: 'While she compares *herself* to the man, she will not compare her *place* and right to his' (my italics).
14. *CD* III/2, p. 313.
15. *CD* III/4, p. 152.
16. E.g. Rosemary Radford Ruether, *Sexism and God-Talk. Towards a Feminist Theology* (SCM Press, London, 1983) pp. 111ff.
17. *CD* III/4, p. 151.
18. A representative objection is made by Elisabeth Schüssler Fiorenza, *In Memory of Her. A Feminist Theological Reconstruction of Christian Origins* (SCM Press, London, 1983), p. 207.
19. *CD* III/2, p. 311.
20. Ibid., pp. 315–6; *CD* III/4, pp. 174–5.
21. *CD* III/2, p. 312.
22. *CD* IV/1, pp. 186–8; II/1, pp. 303–4, 313–15.
23. *CD* I/1, pp. 218–21, 407–8.
24. *CD* I/2, p. 191.
25. *CD* III/2, p. 314.
26. *CD* III/4, p. 155.
27. Joan Arnold Romero, 'The Protestant Principle', in *Religion and Sexism. Images of Woman in the Jewish and Christian Traditions*, ed. R.R. Ruether (Simon & Schuster, New York, 1974), p. 323.
28. *CD* I/1, pp. 168–9. Also see Karl Barth, *Evangelical Theology: An Introduction*, trans. G. Foley (Weidenfeld and Nicholson, London, 1963), p. 23: 'Theology must listen and reply'.
29. *CD* I/1, p. 140; II/1, p. 281; II/2, p. 6; IV/1, p. 80.
30. See e.g. *CD* II/2, pp. 5–6, 101ff.; III/1, pp. 50–1. Cf. Karl Barth, *The Humanity of God*, trans. C.D. Deans (Collins, London, 1961), p. 50: 'In [Christ] the fact is once and for all established that God does not exist without man.' This theme plays a central part in the valuable discussion of Barth's theology in Eberhard Jüngel, *The Doctrine of the Trinity: God's Being is in Becoming*, trans. H. Harris (Scottish Academic Press, Edinburgh, 1975); especially see pp. 72f., 96ff.
31. *CD* III/4, p. 156.
32. Ibid., p. 171.
33. Charlotte Von Kirschbaum, *Der Dienst der Frau in der Wortkündigung*, Theol. Stud. 31, ed. Karl Barth (Evangelischer Verlag, Zürich, 1953).
34. *CD* III/2, p. 311.
35. *CD* III/4, p. 162.
36. Ibid., p. 172.
37. *CD* III/1, pp. 195–6; III/4, pp. 323–4. Dietrich Bonhoeffer had already made this exegesis, but did not relate the male–female relationship to the triune relationships in God: see his *Creation and*

Fall (1932–33), trans. J. C. Fletcher and repr. in *Creation and Temptation* (SCM Press, London, 1966), pp. 37–9.

38. *CD* I/1, p. 370.
39. Ibid., p. 350.
40. *CD* II/1, p. 103.
41. *CD* III/1, p. 196.
42. *CD* I/1, pp. 351, 366, 381.
43. *CD* III/4, p. 161.
44. Ibid., pp. 155–6, 174.
45. Ibid., p. 155.
46. The original study was by Morna D. Hooker, 'Authority on her Head. An Examination of 1 Cor. xi.10', *New Testament Studies* 10 (1963–4), pp. 410–16. In agreement are E. Schüssler Fiorenza, op. cit., p. 230 and C.K. Barrett, *A Commentary on the First Epistle to the Corinthians* (A. & C. Black, London, 1968), pp. 253–5.
47. *CD* III/4, p. 164.
48. I have discussed this point more fully in my article, ' "Woman's Head is Man": A Doctrinal Reflection Upon a Pauline Text', in *The Baptist Quarterly* XXXI (1986), pp. 370–83.
49. Ruether, op. cit., p. 113.

10

The Virgin Mary
and the Feminist Quest

Ann Loades

Mary the mother of Jesus has been the focus of an extraordinary amount of piety and theology down the centuries, and whatever it is she represents has been and remains central to the vitality of Christianity in many parts of the world. It would be worthwhile to try to understand that quite apart from the phenomenon of feminist theology. Mary is also, inevitably, a focus of discussion in inter-church dialogue – indeed, this particular discussion of my own had its origin in an invitation to me from the Oxford branch of the Ecumenical Society of the Blessed Virgin Mary, which requires of its members only that they should be prepared to say or sing the *Magnificat*, though it is a society unlikely to concern itself with feminism as a post-1960s movement, or with feminist theology. As an ecumenical society it will be unable to avoid that concern indefinitely, so long as women alert to feminist and feminist theological concerns continue to make the effort to participate in Christian institutional structures, or Christian societies. One recent attempt to contribute to ecumenical dialogue, with attention to women and their status in mind, is Pope John Paul II's Sixth Encyclical, *Redemptoris Mater* (Mother of the Redeemer) published on 25th March, 1987, to initiate the Marian year which began on Pentecost Sunday, 7th June, 1987, and which concluded on the Feast of Assumption, 15th August, 1988. The Feast, incidentally, survived the Reformation to remain in Oxford University's Calendar, though since it falls in the middle of the long vacation, it is not the focus or occasion of particular celebration, no doubt to the great relief of at least some of the Canons of Christ Church, at once college chapel and diocesan cathedral.

It may be helpful to make a statement about how this present writer sees the enterprise of feminist theology, before turning to my exploration of how Mary is now viewed by a variety of feminist and other theologians, moving along a spectrum from the extremely hostile to the more constructive – none of which falls along strictly denominational lines in any necessary way, so far as one can see. Feminist theologians within the Christian tradition have an argument with that tradition and its values for them in their present culture. If we agree to define feminism at its most minimal as a movement which seeks change for the better in terms of justice for women, it is obvious that a feminist theologian need not be female by sex; and not every female theologian is a feminist theologian. The major feminist theologians at the present time are female, however, because a primary need for women is being expressed in this form of theology, that is, self-reliance in understanding themselves and their relationship to the God they have found to be theirs although mediated to them by a religious tradition which causes some of their problems. They are concerned to use gender analysis to examine the way religious traditions work, the symbolism they use, the characteristics of roles within them, the way religious traditions reflect social assumptions and shape and re-shape those assumptions, and especially the gender-related way in which we talk about divine reality. Theology is itself one such gender-related term, reflecting the unease about the association of the female and the feminine with the godlike. Feminist theologians hope that some of the old stories can be re-told and new ones invented to verbalise God in an inclusively human manner, which takes account of female human beings and what particular societies, including Christian ones, make of the biological differences which render some of us female and some of us male. The languages which mediate divine reality to us have differed depending on their relationship to shifting contexts, and feminist theologians want to imitate the motivation of those who have re-deployed the language, and perhaps even re-use some of the content. The point of the whole endeavour is to try to get us to make an imaginative and moral shift, so that we can come to share a new vision of goodness and be given and gain access to it. This is hardly a destructive or unworthy goal, though the route there may be a painful one. For so far as feminist theologians are concerned, it is not just the biblical texts, but centuries of habits of exegesis, ecclesiastical practice and tradition which are now ripe for scrutiny, all alike without immunity of any kind. And this includes the texts and traditions and devotions about Mary.

Feminist theology is young, but women have been engaged in the re-evaluation of texts and traditions for some time. For instance, one Eliza Sharples in 1832 addressed a meeting, in the course of which she said:

> The tyrant God, Necessity, said to the subject man: 'Of the tree of knowledge of good and evil thou shalt not eat'. Sweet and fair Liberty stepped in . . . spurned the order . . . of the tyrant. 'She took of the fruit thereof, and did eat, and gave also unto her husband with her, and he did eat.' Do you not, with one voice exclaim, well done woman! LIBERTY FOR EVER! If that was a fall, sirs, it was a glorious fall, and such a fall as is now wanted . . . I will be such an Eve, so bright a picture of liberty.[1]

And twelve years later, in 1844, reformer Emma Martin, who once lectured on 'The Holy Ghost, HER Nature, Offices and Laws' (presumably without the benefit of the Syrian Fathers) remarked, 'I have asked the *learned* (?) clergy for rational answers to knotty questions . . . they won't (sic) answer them because they are asked by a *woman*, yet they obtained Christ from the same source. I wonder they did not object to *him* on that account.'[2]

The doyenne of the movement as a whole is Elizabeth Cady Stanton, veteran of the nineteenth century's anti-slavery campaign as well as of other battles, passionately concerned as she was about women's needs and their expression in society. In her eighties, she and a team of colleagues produced a collection of comments on the parts of the Bible which explicitly refer to women, published in 1895 and 1898 as *The Woman's Bible*, and in a new paperback edition in 1985.[3] It is convenient to pick up a passage from *The Woman's Bible*, which represents a not untypical reaction to the 1854 dogma of the 'Immaculate Conception', a dogma not only profoundly troublesome to women, but also, given its long and contentious history, to the relationship between the Roman Catholic Church and other Churches, not just Protestant ones but Orthodox too. This will give us a line of connection to the present-day feminist critique. For the dogma states that:

> the Blessed Virgin Mary, in the first instant of her conception, has been, by a special grace and privilege of Almighty God, and in view of the merits of Jesus Christ, the Saviour of the human race, preserved and exempted from every stain of original sin . . .[4]

We could cite here as a commentary, as it were, *Redemptoris Mater*:

> In the liturgy the church salutes Mary of Nazareth as the church's own beginning, for in the event of the immaculate conception the church sees projected and anticipated in her most noble member, the saving grace of Easter.[5]

In *The Woman's Bible* there is a comment from one of Elizabeth Cady Stanton's collaborators, which muddles two doctrines together, but nevertheless manages to make a point about the way in which this doctrine is still 'heard' and 'read' by women no matter what is said to them about what the doctrines are supposed to mean, that is, excluding women's meanings. Elizabeth Cady Stanton's collaborator seems to have written in some desperation from within a context of hopelessly idealised maternalism when she wrote that:

> I think that the doctrine of the Virgin birth as something higher, sweeter, nobler than ordinary motherhood, is a slur on all the natural motherhood of the world. I believe that millions of children have been as immaculately conceived, as purely born, as was the Nazarene. Why not? Out of this doctrine, and that which is akin to it, have sprung all the monasteries and nunneries of the world, which have disgraced and distorted and demoralised manhood and womanhood for a thousand years. I place beside

the false, monkish, unnatural claim of the Immaculate Conception my mother, who was as holy in her motherhood as was Mary herself.[6]

Leaving aside for the moment the problems raised by Christian asceticism at its awful worst rather than at its splendid best, it is important to be honest about the way in which, as this writer has suggested, doctrines about Mary are consistently assessed by women (even when some kind of theoretical or doctrinal understanding seems to have been achieved) as suggesting the denigration of all other women who are mothers, or even just of all other women, mothers or not. As Edward Schillebeeckx so disastrously exclaimed, 'It is clear that she must be a creature of matchless wonder, this *Immaculat* and *Assumpta*, with whom even the most physically and spiritually beautiful women in the world cannot in any way be compared . . .'[7]

Even without expressly defined dogma, in Orthodox tradition we may be invited to 'stand with reverence in the house of our God, and cry aloud: Hail, Queen of the world; hail, Mary, sovereign over all of us; hail, thou who alone art blameless and fair among women . . .'[8] which may prompt a question about what all other women, as distinct from men, are being blamed for. Being first to sin could be part of the answer. And the *Te Deum* sung at Anglican Matins includes as a reflection on the divine self-emptying, 'When thou tookest upon thee to deliver man / thou didst not abhor the Virgin's womb'. Why 'abhor'? Why should any woman's womb and body be thought of as a possible source of abhorrence? Quite apart from the astonishing prurience displayed in devotion to Mary on the part of some of her adherents,[9] not the least remarkable feature of the Christian tradition is the extreme rarity of the sane comment made by the ninth century Ratramnus, attempting to combat beliefs consequent upon the assumption that the womb was impure, when he insisted firstly that no creature was created vile, and so, also, that 'a woman's uterus is not indecent, but honourable'.[10] He lost his argument.

Luther's attitude to women and to the feminine is somewhat complex, including what Jean Bethke Elshtain calls the 'institutional moment' of his masculinisation of theology – his assault on 'mother' church, and his loss of 'a female linked transcendent moment',[11] notwithstanding his personal devotion to Mary:

> She is my love, the noble Maid,
>   Forget her can I never;
> Whatever honour men have paid,
>   My heart she has for ever.[12]

To the present purpose what matters is his defence of the goodness of sexual desire, which led him to comment on Crotus, who

> wrote blasphemously about the marriage of priests, declaring that the most holy bishop of Mainz was irritated by no annoyance more than by the stinking, putrid, private parts of women. That godless knave, forgetful of his mother and sister, dares to blaspheme God's creature through whom he was himself born. It would be tolerable if he were to find fault with the behaviour of women, but to defile their creation and nature is most godless. As if I were to ridicule a man's face on account of his nose! For the nose is the latrine of man's head and stands above his mouth![13]

Not the most helpful analogy in the circumstances, but the general point stands. And for sheer punitive nastiness, there is little to beat the comment made by Suarez in 1584, who wrote of that 'troublesome weariness with which all pregnant women are burdened, she alone did not experience who alone conceived without pleasure'.[14] Another gem from the writings of a seventeenth-century male saint observes that 'It is a subject of humiliation of all the mothers of children of Adam to know that while they are with child, they carry within them an infant . . . who is the enemy of God, the object of his hatred and malediction and the shrine of the demon.'[15] This is at once a 'theological' response to the sheer difficulties of childbearing, from pregnancy, through birth to lactation and weaning, the risks to the mother, and to the high mortality rate common to children apart from those born in privileged societies, as well as being a preface to the assertion of the need for 're-birth' by baptism, normally male-administered.

What it may also express to women is the theology of 'God punished women more', which in the nineteenth and early twentieth centuries hindered the use of anaesthetic and analgesic drugs in childbirth even when these had become comparatively safe and available. Women were not seen as related to the new 'Eve', nor helped to experience birth as she may have done, relatively without pain and distress, a point made by Leonardo Boff, when he suggests that Mary was free not from pain itself, but from the way we have pain.[16]

If Elizabeth Cady Stanton is the doyenne of the nineteenth-century movement in feminist theology, Mary Daly is the doyenne of the twentieth-century one. Mary Daly indeed acknowledges that despite some elements of the tradition, Mary has been for many women their only symbol of hope, not least when they have been on what she calls 'spiritual starvation rations'[17] – which includes those of the Protestant tradition, eliminating not only Mary 'the apostle to the apostles', but Mary the mother of Jesus and such women saints as there were, from view. Before turning to Mary Daly's pungent comments on Mary the mother of Jesus, however, it is worth noticing that she is herself the product of the North American Roman Catholic tradition which by the time of the Second Vatican Council included some of the most formidably well-educated women in the USA. And to illuminate her exasperation with her original Communion, and that of other women with Christian institutions, we could refer to the documents of the Second Vatican Council,[18] and pay some attention to what they do and do not say about women, as about Mary, because apart from one or two distinctively Roman Catholic touches, the documents are not untypical of Christian attitudes to women.

The documents cut Mary down to size. In Leonardo Boff's book, *The Maternal Face of God*, he summarises various routes into Mariology, the second of which was the one followed by the Council. In the words of Boff's summary, 'Mary never lived in or for herself. Mary was a woman ever at the service of others – of God, of Christ, of redemption, of the Church, of the ultimate meaning of history.' From this perspective, Mary is never to be the subject of a theological consideration of her own, but finds her place in other theological treatises.[19] This feminine non-entity is purportedly rescued from redundancy by the claim that 'Our Lady is the creature who realised to a super-eminent degree whatever values are being discussed or mediated.' The language of perfection is thus largely transferred to the Church, a somewhat problematical move, but as Anne Carr comments in her book *Transforming Grace*,[20] Mary is still in contrast with 'Eve' – all other women – and it does not take much expertise to discover how they are to be viewed.

In some respects the documents of the Council are extremely promising. One of the few explicit references to women indeed regrets that fundamental personal rights are not universally honoured for women, such as the right and freedom to choose a husband, embrace a state of life, or acquire an education or cultural benefits equal to those recognised for men. And Pope Paul VI in International Women's Year in 1975 said that what is most urgent is 'to labour everywhere to have discovered, respected and protected the rights and prerogatives of every woman in her life – educational, professional, civic, social, religious – whether single or married'.[21] Paragraph 52 of The Church Today, on 'the nobility of marriage and the family', to its credit affirms that if the life of the family is to flower it needs kindly communion of minds and painstaking co-operation of the parents in the education of their children. But there is no sense that things could be different and indeed better in what follows.

> The active presence of the father is highly beneficial to their formation. The children, especially the younger among them, need the care of their mother at home. This domestic role of *hers* [my emphasis] must be safely preserved, though the legitimate social progress of women should not be underrated on that account.

What the writers miss is the *essential* active presence of a father to his children, not least to his daughter(s), and the effects on women of their continued restriction to the 'private', as distinct from the public and political, realms, reinforced by suburban housing patterns; not to mention the massive double work burden many of them carry for a very long time, inside their homes in 'unpaid' work, and outside their homes in paid employment, necessary if their families are not to fall into poverty. And in societies where the family is still the economic unit, some 50 per cent of the Third World's food is produced by women, including their work at the heavy agricultural labour involved. How then are women to read not only the documents of the Council, but the words of *Redemptoris Mater*?

> In the light of Mary, the church sees in the face of women the reflection of a beauty which mirrors the loftiest sentiments of which the human heart is capable: the self-offering totality of love; the strength that is capable of bearing the greatest sorrows; limitless fidelity and tireless devotion to work; the ability to combine penetrating intuition with words of support and encouragement.

Women's well-being may well depend upon their finding at least some of these characteristics less than unambiguously praiseworthy.

In Section 60 of the Council's assessment of 'The Church Today', it is indeed acknowledged that women are now employed in almost every area of life, so that it is deemed appropriate 'that they should be able to assume their full proper role *in accordance with their own nature*' (my emphasis). Given the peculiar association of women, rather than men, with nature, it seems to be understood that women's nature is both well defined and limiting, though there is an implicit concession to new possibilities in the need for everyone to 'acknowledge and favour the proper and necessary participation of women in cultural life', and other options seem to be indicated in the sentence added during the final drafting to paragraph 9 of the document on the laity, in the section on 'the various fields of the apostolate', pointing out the importance of women's participation in the various fields of the Church's apostolate. Readers are no doubt meant to be reassured by the footnote which draws attention to the point that this is one of the few places in all the council documents where special attention is given to the contribution of women to the mission of the Church, though it was clearly (to whom?) the mind of the Council that they were included 'and eminently so', whenever the general role of the laity was discussed. The note adds that by the time the Council ended, twelve lay and ten 'religious' women were present as 'auditrices', though not of course what Anne Carr records, that no woman was allowed to read a paper before the assembly (cf. 1 Timothy 2.12, presumably), and that attempts were made to try to bar women journalists from attending council masses or receiving communion during its meetings.[22] Real exasperation could be provoked by the closing messages of the Council, messages to men (males) regarded in terms of their diversified contributions to society, with women having a message addressed to them alone, and as is typical in Christianity, with reference to their sexual states.[23] Women are addressed as girls, wives, mothers and widows, as consecrated virgins, and women living alone, though with the acknowledgment that they constitute half of the immense human family, and with the claim that the Church has 'glorified and liberated' them, a claim not without weight, notwithstanding this present reading of the Council's documents. Women are associated with 'the protection of the home', with cradles and deaths (cf. the nativity and crucifixion scenes?). Mothers are exhorted to 'pass on to your sons and daughters the traditions of your fathers' – mothers not having any? Women are invited to reconcile men with life, to guard purity, unselfishness and piety, to aid men to retain courage in *their* great undertakings, with women's own concern to be particularly with the peace of the world. They are clearly excluded from the address to 'workers' – 'very loved sons', with its sense of unease, mistrust and lack of understanding between the institution and the workers.

It was in response to the Council that one of the most important books in feminist theology appeared in 1968, Mary Daly's *The Church and the second sex*, and the invitation to write that book was prompted by an article of hers which was published in 1965 when she already had a doctorate in theology from Fribourg University in Switzerland, where she was studying philosophy. Mary Daly and Rosemary Radford Reuther were crucial in forming the women's caucus within the American Academy of Religion, at which they both delivered important papers in 1971. Rosemary Radford Reuther's was to appear as 'Misogynism and virginal feminism in the fathers of the church', available with other useful essays in the collection she edited called *Religion and Sexism: Images of Women in the Jewish and Christian Traditions* (1974).[24] Mary Daly's much reprinted essay had a deliberately menacing title: 'Theology after the demise of God the Father; a call for the castration of sexist religion', and she was to part company with Christianity in the course of writing *Beyond God the Father* (1973), now re-issued with an 'Original Reintroduction'. One also needs to read *Gyn/Ecology* (1978)[25] and *Pure Lust* (1984)[26], each of which contains devastating attacks on Christianity's core symbolism. Tucked away in a footnote of *Beyond God the Father* is her assessment of Phyllis Trible's paper of 1973 on 'Depatriarchalizing in Biblical Tradition', on which Mary Daly commented that 'It might be interesting to speculate upon the probable length of a "depatriarchalized Bible". Perhaps there would be enough salvageable material to comprise an interesting pamphlet'.[27] It is relevant to bear this in mind particularly when we attend to her treatment of the story of the Annunciation.

For Mary Daly, Mary is killed by the dogmas about her, killed, though apparently alive, like a dolled-up Christmas tree. She points out that the 1854 definition (which was in the forefront of the attention of Elizabeth Cady Stanton's collaborator's mind) coincides with the first wave of feminism, though it is in fact doubtful that the definition was *aimed* at feminism. Here is a woman preserved from original sin by the grace of her son not only in advance of *his* birth but of her own. As *Redemptoris Mater* puts it, 'together with the Father, the Son has chosen her, entrusting her eternally to the Spirit of holiness . . .'. What she is purified from is her own autonomous being; her psyche is already dismembered; and the story of the Annunciation affirming her need of male acceptance – 'according to thy will' – makes her doubly a victim. She can then function only as a token woman of hope, since she stands over against the incompetence and array of weaknesses ascribed to women in general. So for Mary Daly, the impossible ideal of Virgin/Mother has ultimately a punitive function, since no actual woman can live up to it, throwing all women back into the status of the first Eve, and essentially reinforcing the universality of women's low-caste status.[28] Yet she acknowledges that the Immaculate Conception could be understood as the negation of the myth of feminine evil, foreshadowing the 'Fall into the sacred . . .

free from the crippling burden of submersion in the role of the Other'.[29]

This is the convenient point to couple with her opinions of the 1854 dogma Mary Daly's treatment of the 1950 dogma of the Assumption: 'The Immaculate Mother of God, Mary ever virgin, having run the course of her earthly life, was taken up body and soul into the glory of heaven . . .'. Edward Yarnold SJ has eloquently pointed out the differences, let us say, between the Assumption as painted by Titian and an icon of the Dormition in the Orthodox tradition, maintaining nonetheless that 'Both sides of Christendom believe that Mary was received body and soul into heaven to be reunited with her Son in glory'.[30] Mary Daly has made the point that the dogma could at long last indicate a 'no' to the peculiar association of women with sin and flesh and matter, and it could also, in the immediate post World War II period, remind us of the importance of bodies, even indeed of Jewish ones. Unfortunately, the dogma's promulgation coincided with a backlash against female independence, not wholly understandable as part of the need to re-found families. For Mary Daly, this dogma then annihilates women's earthly presence, and rehabilitates her as defeated, eliminated from public life, saved, once again, by the male.[31] Given her assessment of the male monogender mating of the Trinity, one could see too what she might make of Leonardo Boff's attempts to secure a special relation of the third 'person' of the Trinity with Mary, Boff breaking well out of the constrictions of the Vatican II documents.

Salvation for women by a God manifested contingently as a male was coped with in earlier periods via the analogy of 'male is to female as form is to matter', an analogy no longer defensible, any more than is an assumption associated with it, that 'the first and principal cause of offspring is always in the father', and here Marina Warner's book on Mary is illuminating. She quotes the passage in Aeschylus' *Oresteia*, where Orestes at his trial cries out in protest, 'And dost thou call *me* a blood relation of my mother?' Apollo arbitrates with the judgment that 'The so-called offspring is not produced by the mother . . . She is not more than the nurse, as it were, of the newly conceived foetus. It is the male who is the author of its being'.[32] This has been untenable without considerable qualification since the development of embryology from the early nineteenth century onwards (and Boff, to his credit, tries to pay attention to this development), but it still influences doctrines about the ministry as it does doctrines about Mary. So in the Bishop of London's November 1985 newsletter he did his best to elaborate the view that 'in the whole of human instinct and understanding it is the masculine which is associated with giving and the feminine with receiving', a piece of gender construction as intolerable for men as it is dishonest about women, and in the latter is liable to produce some hilarity in those who have become aware of and articulate about their role in securing the well-being of men without any firm expectation that the converse will obtain. In Marian doctrines, we can still see the influence of this theory, which has to do with what a culture thinks reproduction is all about, that is 'the relationship between procreative beliefs and the wider context (world view, cosmology, culture) in which they are found'.[33] Paternity, in Carol Delaney's analysis, has meant 'the primary, essential and creative role' in reproduction, and the meaning of maternity as 'nurture' is epitomised by Mary.

Carol Delaney takes the root meaning of 'virgin birth' (and we may add the dogmas already mentioned) to be a version of *folk* theories about procreation, the essential implication of which is that a child originates from only *one* source, and so is entirely consistent with theological monotheism. Her fieldwork in a Turkish Muslim village enabled her to identify an appropriate theory of procreation, which is that 'The male is said to plant the seed and the woman is said to be like a field', so the woman's role is secondary, supportive and nurturant. So she identifies a further analogy, of 'Woman is to Man as the created, natural world is to God', and we connect this again with metaphors from the Orthodox liturgy quoted earlier. First:

> Then the power of the Most High overshadowed her that knew not wedlock, so that she might conceive: and he made her fruitful womb as a fertile field for all who long to reap the harvest of salvation, singing: Alleluia![34]

Second, we find Mary urged by the unborn John in Elizabeth's womb to rejoice as the 'vine with unwithering shoot', 'farm with untainted fruit', 'arable yielding a bountiful stack of pity', 'furbishing a lush pasturage'.[35]

Carol Delaney is surely correct to point out that the knowledge that women are co-engenderers, co-creators, providing half the 'seed' so to speak, half the genetic constitution of the child in addition to pregnancy, birth and suckling, has not yet been encompassed symbolically. Paternity is indeed a cultural construction of a powerful kind, and one cannot simply claim that the meaning of Mary's virginity is that 'the role played by the human race in the Incarnation is simply that of accepting God's gift as a gift and as a grace, and nothing more',[36] yet another gender construction associating receptivity with the feminine and giving with the masculine. Though there is something important to hold on to here for our culture, as Lochman wrote in his comment on how Mr Fix-It is set aside, for humanity in the Incarnation is involved 'in the form *not* of a primarily creating, controlling, self-assertive, self-glorifying humanity but as a primarily listening, receiving, serving and blessed ("graced") human being', as Mary is impressively described in the Christmas narrative.[37] *Redemptoris Mater*, however, returns us firmly to gender construction, influenced apparently by a particular school of psychology, when the text says that in Mary's faith, first at the annunciation and then fully at the foot of the cross, 'an interior space was reopened within humanity which the eternal Father can fill "with every spiritual blessing" . . .'.

One needs also to look at another strand in the tradition, which has to do with the point that early Christianity offered women who did not or could not fulfil certain socio-sexual roles a new kind of aspiration,[38] and for them, the *virgin* Mary was a possible symbol of that discipleship which took overriding priority in their lives. For to be sexually virginal was to be freed from a measure of male domination, to be unexploited and unexploitable, to enjoy a certain sense of transcendence as an element of personhood, so sexual asceticism was not necessarily imposed on women as a kind of constraint. This is an important and neglected possibility in the Protestant tradition. Even Mary Daly acknowledges this, when she writes that the doctrine that Mary was a virgin before, during and after the birth of Jesus, 'by its very absurdity . . . literally screams that biology and abstinence from sexual activity are *not* the essential dimensions of the symbol of Mary as a virgin . . . '.[39] The doctrine may be saying something about female autonomy to women, about the possibility of women's relation to divine reality without male mediation, although there is a further problem about the metaphors used to indicate the divine that would have to be tackled at this as at other points of Christian doctrine. And Mary Daly and others may be mistaken about the possibility of enjoying transcendence and autonomy without the necessity for sexual virginity or chastity, depending on how sexual relationships are construed and function in a particular society. Sarah Maitland's brilliant novel *Daughter of Jerusalem* (1978) catches this element of virginity beautifully in her initial reflection on Mary, small, dark, devout, probably illiterate, unconventional, of unassailable self-assurance:

> Of course her assent is a sexual act, she tried to explain, pushing her hair back under her scarf, and grinding her bare toes into the coarse sand, because it was complete, it was made with the whole of her being. It was an assent to the totality of herself, to a womanhood so vital and empowered that it could break free of biology and submission, any dependence on or need for a masculine sexuality – that furrow in which the crop of women's sex has been held to be rooted.[40]

One extremely important manifestation of this sense of 'womanhood' was that it made the pursuit of learning possible, even if it often meant retreat from the public world into the seclusion of the book-lined cell – not the worst of all fates. Helen Waddell might be approximately a good twentieth-century example, daughter of an Irish Presbyterian missionary family as she was, even though reading the sympathetic biography of her by Dame Felicitas Corrigan may still leave one with a sense of regret for a life not entirely fulfilled. But consider, for example, what is expressed in her translation of a ninth-century lament for a young abbess, a translation made during the bombing raids of September 1941, which makes it all the more poignant:

Thou hast come safe to port,
    I still at sea,
The light is on thy head,
    Darkness in me.
Pluck thou in heaven's field
    Violet and rose
Whilst I strew flowers that will thy vigil keep,
Where thou dost sleep,
    Love, in thy last repose.[41]

And we could add to that her translation of an eleventh-century verse about the virgins in the fields of the blessed, the girls illustrated as it were in Fra Angelico's picture of St Thomas Aquinas and St Bonaventura conversing in Paradise together:

Gertrude, Agnes, Prisca, Cecily,
Lucia, Thekla, Petronel,
Agatha, Barbara, Juliana,
Wandering there in the fresh spring meadows,
Looking for flowers to make them a garland,
Roses red of the Passion,
Lilies and violets for love.[42]

We have forgotten why it was that virginity could signal a vocation, and this forgetfulness has in part to do with its praise by undoubted woman-haters, even making the most generous allowances in the interpretation of the rhetoric of misogyny. For virginity may be associated also with stony *a*sexuality, and the bizarre behaviour which can accompany it, the product of a tradition which deemed women not to be as godlike as men are, approximating to godlikeness only in so far as they approximate to masculinity. When males are taken to be the normative and representative and essentially life-giving expression of the human species, with females as defective, imperfect and merely nuturant human beings, then virginity changes its meaning, and signifies the approximation to an ideal one can never reach. One manifestation of this is the phenomenon of anorexia, the inability to eat, not necessarily a religious or indeed peculiarly Christian phenomenon, but undoubtedly present in those women with a passion for what they took to be moral and spiritual perfection – *vir*ility and *vir*tue – an approximation to that image of deity they might be thought not to bear in their own right. The asceticism necessary for the pursuit of their virginal vocation sometimes tipped them into uncontrollable anorexia and so to amenorrhea, not least where they were in rebellion against the dependent forms of Christianity on offer to women. Getting control of her body in asceticism however extreme, retrieves a woman from the sense of helplessness she experiences simply by virtue of being female. It commands attention, and for a time, tremendous energy, as well as the ability to by-pass religious controls, find communion with the deity, and criticise popes and archbishops.

The search for transcendence here can tip women into near or actual half-unconscious destruction as petrified living dead.[43] If, however, we could retrieve the association of 'virgin' with autonomy, but carefully balanced with a sense of co-inherence, and without the abasement of a woman's visual image;[44] and if we could by-pass sugary sweetness and dizzy immobilisation on a pedestal, then Mary might be re-associated with the affirmation and not the negation of what women discover themselves to be, and we might re-connect Mary to present needs as, for example, Rosemary Radford Reuther attempts to do.[45]

She, like Mary Daly, wants female presence acknowledged without fear of real women, a fear not always unjustifiable; she wants the co-ordination of nature and grace recovered for those whose ecclesiastical traditions have lost it – again, arguably expressed in Mary's rapturous assent. Arguing that we cannot remain with a doctrine of salvation mediated by the male alone, she asks for the genuine reciprocity of women and men together in the Churches, an expression of the way in which the female plays a co-operating role in the work of salvation. This could have important consequences outside the Church too, in the support each person gives to the dignity and self-actualisation of the other. We could connect with this ideal of 'reciprocity' a remark of C.S. Lewis's – astonishingly, since he is not frequently associated with perceptive comments about the reciprocity of men and women together, of a kind which women can recognise as being supportive to them. Yet perhaps as a result of his life with Joy Davidman he was to write after her death:

> It is arrogance in us to call frankness, fairness and chivalry 'masculine' when we see them in a woman; it is arrogance in them to describe a man's sensitiveness or tact or tenderness as 'feminine'. But also what poor, warped fragments of humanity most mere men and mere women must be to make the implications of that arrogance plausible.[46]

And it is Lewis, too, who anticipated in a way the appropriation of Mary for 'liberation' theology, writing of Jesus as very much his mother's son, in his *Reflections on the Psalms*:

> There is a fierceness, even a touch of Deborah, mixed with the sweetness in the *Magnificat* to which most painted Madonnas do little justice; matching the frequent severity of His own sayings. I am sure that the private life of the holy family was, in many senses, 'mild' and 'gentle', but perhaps hardly in the way some hymn writers have in mind. One may suspect, on proper occasions, a certain astringency; and all in what people at Jerusalem regarded as a rough north-country accent.[47]

Rosemary Radford Reuther ties the *Magnificat* in to the revolutionary spirit of liberation theology (a possibility obliterated for centuries by the practice of having it sung by pre-pubescent boys in skirts and frills) with women above all representing the 'nobodies' made to be persons as a result of the self-emptying of divine power in Jesus. Anne Carr makes Mary herself a symbol of the transformed world for which women hope, edging away from Mary as the impossible double-bind figure identified by Mary Daly. Anne Carr acknowledges that Mary *is* a utopian figure, a mystery. 'Her intimate place in the Christian pattern enables us to imagine a healed, reconciled, finally transformed world. While it is God who works human salvation in Christ, and the Spirit who inspires the active response of the Church, it is Mary who is the sign of the final transformation of the world.'[48]

There remain, however, a number of less 'orthodox' possibilities.

Marina Warner[49] and Mary Daly[50] both spot something else in Mary which makes her important to women by exhausted imperceptive moralism, and this was something explained, oddly enough, in *The Times* of 7th February, 1987, by Rabbi Ephraim Gastwirth, though he evidently disapproves of what he describes, preferring, rather, 'the love and fear of a stern father'. For mother, he tells us, has a love which is eternal and her broad arms encompass all her children without distinction. 'Indeed, her love is often stronger for the weak and wayward child, seeking to ensure his survival and to keep him within the family group. The mother's love is unconditional.' The point is that there is a sense in which Mary is as splendidly unconventional as Jesus was, since her loyalty to her own explodes the bounds of strict justice, as Marina Warner makes clear. 'Through her, the whole gay crew of wanton, loving, weak humanity finds its way to paradise.' So Marina Warner quotes the devils who say, 'Heaven's the place for all the riff-raff / We've got the wheat and God the chaff.'[51] This association of Mary with unconventional love and with self-determination, could relate her back to some less hallowed women, taking a clue from the genealogy of the First Gospel – women such as Ruth, Tamar, Rahab and Bathsheba, all specially related to messianic promise,[52] as well as to some of the thoroughly idiosyncratic women of the apostolic tradition. We would recall that Elizabeth's greeting, 'Blessed art thou among women', recalls comparable blessings to both Jael and Judith, before paying close attention also to the woman who wiped Jesus' feet with her hair, to the Syro-Phoenician woman who argues it out with him as does Martha in the Fourth Gospel, the Samaritan woman of the same Gospel, first missionary despite her past, and Mary of Magdala, not that figment of ecclesiastical imagination, a reformed prostitute, but someone healed of 'demonic' illness by Jesus. This 'apostle to the apostles' proclaims the resurrection as did the mother of the Maccabean martyrs, and is followed by Phoebe the deacon, Junia, given apostolic acknowledgment by Paul, and many others. And Elisabeth Moltmann-Wendel has made a particularly interesting reassessment of tradition about Mary,[53] pleading for much more honesty about its biblical origins, with the limitations imposed by that origin, and makes us see Mary as a 'living, critical, angry unadapted mother', just as difficult as some of the other people around Jesus, men as well as women. She emphasises that Mary needs to take her place, perhaps a pre-eminent place, but only one place, among all these other 'sisters'. Elisabeth Moltmann-Wendel suggests that one of the greatest defects of the tradition, even with the presence of at least some women saints available, has been its monolithic character, the attempt to load into just one symbol much of what women can represent in human life, to men primarily, but with women finding in Mary possibilities for themselves. Feminist theologians who follow Elisabeth Moltmann-Wendel's lead will not want Mary confined by ecclesiastical definition however subtle, but want to be able to relate Mary to other women and the multiplicity of vocations and possibilities of their lives now and in the future. So if, and only if, women want to find role models in biblical and non-biblical tradition, Mary may still have something to offer.

Elisabeth Moltmann-Wendel made a proposal, 'Becoming human in new community', at the World Council of Churches meeting in Sheffield, in June 1981, 'The community of women and men in the Church', the proceedings of which were edited by Constance Parvey.[54] In her report on the meeting, Constance Parvey drew special attention to the fact that Mary had been singled out as one of the basic paradigms, not least in the section on tradition and traditions. She wrote that Mary is seen as a sharing woman seeking out Elizabeth to tell the news of her pregnancy; as being in the tradition of prophecy; neglected by her son in favour of his mission; and as a disciple journeying in partnership with Jesus along with other women and men. 'Then we witness her profound grief at the death of her child under the judgement of religious and political powers, her faithfulness to follow him to the tomb, and the divine gift bestowed upon her to be a witness of the resurrection of the "flesh of her flesh, the bone of her bone".' Here is no model of submission and subordination, but someone fully living out her partnership with God in the Christ event.[55]

Between the present and the fulfilment of Anne Carr's vision, there are elements here which could be extremely valuable to those who still find their resources in the Christian tradition in relation to the appalling circumstances of their lives, as well as in hope for blessing and flourishing.

This essay represents a stage in exploration and does not attempt to do more than indicate some options. For the present writer, the least that could be said about Mary is that she represents what novelist Robertson Davies suggests in his phrase 'having the body in the soul's keeping',[56] but also, that 'Grace is not faceless', to quote Cornelius Ernst OP.[57] The material drawn on towards the end of the essay, however, would edge us towards meaning for that phrase rather more incarnated in women's lives than theology has so far been prepared to concede.

NOTES

1. Quoted in B. Taylor, *Eve and the New Jerusalem* (Virago, London, 1983), p. 146.
2. Ibid., p. 153.
3. Elizabeth Cady Stanton, *The Woman's Bible* (Polygon, Edinburgh, 1985).
4. Cited from K. Rahner, *Theological Investigations* (Darton, Longman and Todd, London, 1961), Vol. 1, p. 201.
5. *Redemptoris Mater*, as published in *Origins: NC Documentary Service*, Vol. xvi:43 (9th April, 1987), pp. 745–67.
6. *Woman's Bible*, p. 114.
7. E. Schillebeeckx, *Mary, Mother of the Redemption* (Sheed and Ward, London, 1964), p. 172.
8. Ecumenical Society of the Blessed Virgin Mary, *The Akathistos Hymn* (Bocardo Press, Oxford, 1987), p. 17.
9. H. Graef, *Mary: a history of doctrine and devotion* (Sheed and Ward, London, 1985), p. 245, quoting from the twelfth-century Amadeus of Lausanne: 'The Holy Spirit will come upon you, that at his touch your womb may tremble and swell, your spirit rejoice and your womb flower . . .'
10. Ibid., p. 176.
11. J.B. Elshtain, 'Luther *Sic* – Luther *Non*', *Theology Today*, Vol. xliii (July 1986), pp. 155–68, pp. 167–8. And see chapter two of her *Meditations on Modern Political Thought: Masculine/Feminine Themes from Luther to Arendt* (Praeger, New York, 1986).
12. V. White, *Soul and Psyche* (Collins, London, 1960), p. 134, quoting the translation of another Dominican, Sebastian Bullough. And see M. Thurian, *Mary, Mother of the Lord, Figure of the Church* (Mowbray,

London, 1985/1963) for more material on the Marian theology and devotion of the Reformers.

13. J.B. Elshtain, *Public Man, Private Woman* (Robertson, Oxford, 1981), p. 87.
14. M. Warner, *Alone of all her sex* (Picador, London, 1985), p. 43.
15. Ibid., p. 57.
16. L. Boff, *The maternal face of God* (Harper and Row, San Francisco, 1987/1979), p. 148.
17. M. Daly, *Beyond God the Father* (Women's Press, London, 1986/1973), p. 81f.
18. W.M. Abbott, ed., *The Documents of Vatican II* (Chapman, London, 1965).
19. Boff, op. cit., pp. 10f.
20. A. Carr, *Transforming Grace: Christian Tradition and Women's Experience* (Harper and Row, San Francisco, 1988), p. 191.
21. Ibid., p. 33.
22. Ibid., p. 30.
23. Abbott, *Documents*, pp. 732–5.
24. R.R. Ruether, ed., *Religion and Sexism: Images of Women in the Jewish and Christian Traditions* (Simon and Schuster, New York, 1974).
25. M. Daly, *Gyn/Ecology* (Women's Press, London 1984).
26. M. Daly, *Pure Lust* (Women's Press, London, 1984).
27. Daly, *Beyond God the Father*, p. 205.
28. Ibid., pp. 81f.
29. Ibid., p. 86.
30. E.Y. Yarnold, *The Assumption*, 1980 Assumption Day Lecture for the Parish Church of St Mary and All Saints, Walsingham.
31. Daly, *Pure Lust*, p. 128.
32. Warner, op. cit., p. 41.
33. C. Delaney, 'The Meaning of Paternity and the Virgin Birth Debate', *Man*, Vol. xxi:3 (1986), pp. 454–513.
34. *Akathistos*, p. 19.
35. Ibid., p. 33.
36. J. McHugh, 'The Virginal Conception of Jesus', paper of 25th October, 1985, published for the ESBVM, p. 6.
37. J.M. Lochman, *The Faith We Confess: an Ecumenical Dogmatics* (Fortress, Philadelphia, 1984), pp. 112–13.
38. R.S. Kraemer, 'The Conversion of Women to Ascetic Forms of Christianity', *Signs*, Vol. vi:2 (1980), pp. 298–307.
39. Daly, *Beyond God the Father*, p. 85.
40. S. Maitland, *Daughters of Jerusalem* (Pavanne, London, 1987), p. 30.
41. Dame F. Corrigan, *Helen Waddell: a Biography* (Gollancz, London, 1986), p. 317.
42. H. Waddell, *The Wandering Scholars* (Penguin, Harmondsworth, 1954), p. 123.

43. See Chapter 3 of A. Loades, *Searching for Lost Coins* (SPCK, London, 1987).

44. Ruether, 'Misogynism' etc. as in note 23, p. 166.

45. R.R. Ruether, *Mary, the Feminine Face of the Church* (SCM, London, 1979); and Chapter 6 of her *Sexism and God-talk: towards a Feminist Theology* (SCM, London, 1983).

46. C.S. Lewis, *A Grief Observed* (Faber, London, 1986), p. 43.

47. C.S. Lewis, *Reflections on the Psalms* (Fontana, London, 1961), p. 13.

48. Carr, *Transforming Grace*, p. 193.

49. Warner, op. cit. her chapter on 'The Hour of our Death'.

50. Daly, *Beyond God the Father*, pp. 91–2.

51. Warner, op. cit., p. 325.

52. R.E. Brown, K.P. Donfried, J.A. Fitzmyer and J. Reumann, eds, *Mary in the New Testament* (Chapman, London, 1978), p. 82; cf. J.C. Anderson, 'Mary's Difference: Gender and Patriarchy in the Birth Narratives', *Journal of Religion*, Vol. lxvii:2 (April 1987), pp. 183–202.

53. E. Moltmann-Wendel, *A Land Flowing with Milk and Honey* (SCM, London, 1986), pp. 193f.

54. C.F. Parvey, ed., *The Community of Women and Men in the Church* (WCC, Geneva, 1983); cf. *The Ecumenical Review*, Vol. xl:1 (January, 1988) for articles developing the community study.

55. Parvey, op. cit., p. 141.

56. R. Davies, *The Rebel Angels* (Penguin, Harmondsworth, 1985), p. 56.

57. C. Ernst, *Multiple Echo* (Darton, Longman and Todd, London, 1979), p. 124.

Patricia and Charles Vereker gave me hospitality when I wrote the first draft of this paper. I am immensely grateful to them, and to audiences in Oxford, Earlham College, Richmond, Indiana, Vanderbilt Divinity School, and especially the Faculties of the Lutheran School of Divinity, Chicago, and Catholic Theological Union, Chicago, for their comments. Professor Herbert Anderson arranged for me to read this paper at CTU, at which I had the privilege of meeting Professor Anne Carr, Professor Dianne Bergant and Professor Carolyn Osiek. Without the hospitality Professors Herbert and Phyllis Anderson gave me whilst in Chicago, this paper would not have developed as it has, and my final thanks are specially to them.

ACKNOWLEDGEMENTS

The authors are grateful for the right to use the two poems on page 171.

'Thou has come safe to port . . .' is reprinted by kind permission of Miss M. Martin.

'Gertrude, Agnes, Prisca, Cecily . . .', by Sigebert of Liege, translated by Helen Waddell in *The Wandering Scholars*, is reprinted by permission of Constable Publishers and © University of Michigan Press.

Other Marshall Pickering paperbacks

The Old Testament in Sociological Perspective

Andrew Mayes

A great deal of recent scholarship on the Old Testament has been
shaped by modern-day sociological studies. In fact, it has been
argued that sociology has replaced historical criticism as the
indispensable basis for approaching the Old Testament. In many
cases, these sociological assumptions have been declared, but in
others they remain hidden, yet have a profound effect on the
writings of those who hold them.

In this important new book, Professor Andrew Mayes looks at
the roots of these sociological methods. He begins by examining
the two major traditions in sociology, tracing them back to their
foundations in Weber and Durkheim. He then goes on to explore
the influence these traditions have had in biblical scholarship,
especially in the highly influential works of Causse, Alt and Noth
earlier in the twentieth century. He also looks at the more recent
sociological studies in early Israelite history and religion.

The purpose of *The Old Testament in Sociological Perspective* is to bring
to the surface the sociological assumptions, implicit and explicit,
which play such a key role in the modern interpretation of the Old
Testament. Professor Mayes examines some of the major
contemporary writings on the subject: Gottwald on pre-monarchic
history and religion; Wilson on prophecy; Hanson on apocalyptic
theology. He suggests an approach to the Old Testament which
can make constructive use of the different sociological approaches
without becoming enslaved to them.

Trade paperback   019379   196 pp